AF601297

Influencing Leaders

Influencing Leaders

The SEVEN DISCIPLINES *of the* TRUSTED STRATEGIC ADVISOR

JAMES E. LUKASZEWSKI
HELIO FRED GARCIA

WILEY

Published by John Wiley & Sons, Inc., Hoboken, New Jersey.

For general information on our other products and services or for technical support, please contact our Customer Care Department within the United States at (800) 762-2974, outside the United States at (317) 572-3993 or fax (317) 572-4002.

Wiley also publishes its books in a variety of electronic formats. Some content that appears in print may not be available in electronic formats. For more information about Wiley products, visit our web site at www.wiley.com.

Library of Congress Cataloging-in-Publication Data is Available:

ISBN 978-1-394-43228-8 (Cloth)
ISBN 978-1-394-43229-5 (ePub)
ISBN 978-1-394-43230-1 (ePDF)

Cover Design: Wiley
Cover Images: © A-R-T-U-R/Getty Images,
© Berezka_Klo/Getty Images
Author Photos: Courtesy of Helio Fred Garcia,
Courtesy of James E. Lukaszewski

Printed and bound by CPI Group (UK) Ltd, Croydon, CR0 4YY

C9781394432288_150626

On becoming the number one Number Two:

To all the Number Twos and those who want to be more significant trusted advisors—the disappointed, frustrated, yet eager and persistent staff people in communications, corporate strategy, finance, human resources, law, IT, business continuation and recovery, compliance, and security who know that if only they could get to the inner circle and be heard, their advice could save the day and avoid career-defining moments for their boss.

This book will help you become the number one Number Two you imagine yourself to be, wherever you work, whether you are an internal expert or an outside consultant. The concepts talked about here will make your professional life richer, more professionally rewarding, and exhilarating.

Working at the top is exciting, intense, and often fraught with confrontation and the clash of big egos and ideas. Some days it is like being in intellectual combat. Winston Churchill once remarked that there is absolutely nothing more invigorating than being shot at, and missed.

Welcome to the line of fire.

Contents

Influencing Leaders: The Seven Disciplines of the Trusted Strategic Advisor

The First Discipline: Be Trustworthy

Trust is the foundation for a relationship between advisor and leader. Learn the 5 components of trust, 5 behaviors to establish trust, and 10 ways to lose trust.

The Second Discipline: Become a Verbal Visionary

Advisors must have powerful verbal skills. Discover the six opportunities advisors have to provide advice verbally, the verbal skill self-assessment, and the six behaviors and actions of verbal visionaries.

The Third Discipline: Develop a Management Perspective

Management advisors need to talk about the boss's goals and objectives. You need to be able to see the business or organization through the leaders' eyes.

The Fourth Discipline: Think Strategically

The concepts and ideas behind being strategic include the seven virtues of a strategist, the four phases of strategic thinking, and the five barriers that hold strategists back. Find out how much of a strategist you are.

The Fifth Discipline: Understand the Power of Patterns, Be a Forecaster

One of the great insights into being a powerful forecaster is understanding how to learn the patterns of past experiences. Learn the five lessons for working with patterns and recognizing threats.

The Sixth Discipline: Advise Constructively

Learn how to structure advice so that you are clearly understood and the boss can act on your advice, pitfalls to giving advice, strategies and techniques to help you structure advice, and three strategic tools to use.

The Seventh Discipline: Show the Boss How to Use Your Advice

Teach the boss how to take and to use your advice, four approaches to providing constructive advice, seven elements of effective advice, and how to assess your daily performance.

Preface

By Jim:

First of all, thank you. It is an honor, privilege, and pleasure to be with you, whether this is the first or forty-first time we have been with each other.

Listen carefully: the mission of *Influencing Leaders* is to end your failed search for that mythical "table" everyone else is also searching for and help YOU BECOME THE TABLE, to live it, believe in it, act like it, and succeed because of it. Being the table is up to you and only you.

Time to abandon the "getting to the table" concept altogether. It's a myth. It's a time waster. It's technically unachievable because such a table doesn't really exist in real life. Besides, executives detest the idea of a table where all internal and external consultants are sitting around. There is a better destination: seeking to be in the inner circle.

You might want to read Chapter 11, "You Are the Table," right now. Then come back here to continue getting on board *Influencing Leaders*.

Review the Table of Contents. Each chapter, read in any order, is a critical ingredient, a leg, you might say, on your table, as you become a truly influential, trusted, and sought after Strategic Advisor.

Be the table no matter how many others there are in the room. When you are in the room alone with the boss, the room is full. **Yes, you can do this**. You will be amazed and surprised as you transform yourself, guided by *Influencing Leaders,* and you find growing acceptance, inclusion, access, relevance, and respect among leaders.

To leaders the reason is obvious. The more you learn to be their table, bosses realize that you are in it for them. Nearly everyone else has an agenda.

What I develop in my relationships with top people are four things:

1. To seek and recommend ideal behavior, to always be truthful and of value whenever I am called to serve.
2. I aspire to be among the first they call when there is trouble or strategic opportunity.
3. I am focused on providing advice on the spot, whatever the circumstance, whatever the time of day, and whatever mistakes happen to be.
4. I want to be the last person the principal speaks to before they walk out from behind the curtain and the klieg lights go on, and it's their career lit up or at risk.

One thing I emphasize to those I advise is what we are really doing when we get in the room where decisions are made. One of the ways I do this—and you can, too—is to focus on providing meaningful options for decision-makers to choose from, or not. Most staff have limited specialized knowledge of their business or organization. Being an options suggester is powerfully helpful and always welcome. One of my most famous thoughts on this is a strategic advice approach called the three-minute drill that you'll learn about in Chapter 9.

The goal of being a trusted advisor is to be in the room when people decide important things, whether or not it's your idea that prevails. Becoming a Trusted Strategic Advisor, much like being a CEO, is mostly on-the-job training and experience.

In reality, very few public relations and public affairs people are in the room frequently enough to have great influence. Many of them behave and sound like they're in the C-Suite every day. Truthfully very few of them actually get past the admin. So they make up things that sound like they were actually telling the boss what to do. Stop doing that. Get in the room. Get invited back. Earn it.

This book is filled with ideas and behaviors to be able to be invited successfully on a daily basis. Being in the room is exciting, often scary, especially when the boss looks at you, points a finger in your direction, and says,

"What would you do, what's the first thing I should do?" Why? What if? So what?

Over the years, I have served more than 300 clients, usually helping CEOs with major problems they brought on themselves and had to essentially recover alone.

I have been a member of, certified by, and made a Fellow by both the Public Relations Society of America (PRSA) and the International Association of Business Communicators (IABC). In return, both organizations, especially PRSA, have given me several decades of platforms to speak from, teach from, learn from, and be listened to. Both organizations have been powerful connectors to those who practice public relations and public affairs at the highest levels in America and around the world.

I am the longest serving (35 years, now emeritus) member of the PRSA Board of Ethics and Professional Standards. I was also among the first in the group accredited by the SCCE (Society of Corporate Compliance and Ethics), a global organization mostly of attorneys engaged in compliance and ethics work as part of their legal practices within organizations.

Friends with large international practices have told me on numerous occasions that wherever you go on the planet to study and use public relations, you'll find something written, spoken, or produced by Jim Lukaszewski. This is an extraordinary thought for a kid from Robbinsdale, Minnesota, who entered the field of public relations at the age of 35.

We hope you find this book practical, helpful, meaningful, wise, and as essential as Fred and I imagined it to be.

Welcome aboard.

Joining me in this edition is Helio Fred Garcia, one of the most amazing practitioners, coaches, and counselors I've ever known. Our professional relationship and friendship has been ongoing for more than 40 years. When you read what he says about me; I could say all those things and more about him. So when I asked his advice about revising *Why Should the Boss Listen to You*, he instantly offered to help crystallize what I started to accomplish 20 years ago: to encourage, to inspire, and increase the acceptance, help, and value of Trusted Strategic Advisors. Their job is to provide essential and powerful assistance to leaders: better ways to think, better ways to act, better ways to strategize, and better ways to achieve whatever the missions, goals, and visions of those they advise.

It was Fred who, in one of our conversations early on, talked about how he uses my earlier book in his classes and with his clients as a way of teaching trusted advisors how to:

- Expand engagement
- Gain acceptance
- Have better access
- Improve impact
- Be included in crucial top-level decision-making
- Improve influence
- Powerfully influence leaders
- Spot those ideas and strategies that are ill advised.

Over the years, Fred has been responsible for getting me engaged in many of the most exciting, interesting, and often scary projects in my career.

This book shares the real wisdom of our combined 80-plus years of experience.

By Fred:

Jim Lukaszewski has been my mentor, friend, collaborator, colleague, teaching partner, writing partner, and inspiration for four decades.

No single person has had a greater or more direct impact on my career than Jim. He took me under his wing when I was just starting out, and he helped me mature as an advisor, communicator, strategist, listener, thinker, and speaker.

Nearly 30 years ago, when I was the faculty recruiter for the New York University School of Professional Studies public relations program, I persuaded Jim to join the NYU faculty, and for 22 years he helped shape the careers of hundreds of our students.

Jim and I have had clients in common. Most clients are confidential. But some include the U.S. Marine Corps and the U.S. Defense Information School, where we once had the pleasure of team teaching and where books by each of us—including the original *Why Should the Boss Listen to You?*—are assigned. We have taught workshops together in the Public Relations Society of America. We have read and provided guidance on the drafts of each other's books. We have helped each other see things from new perspectives. And because I've been following in Jim's footsteps, we've even, at times, received the same recognition. For example, in 2010 Jim was awarded the Public Relations Society of America—New York's John W. Hill Award for lifetime achievement. I was surprised and honored to receive the same award in 2021.

When Jim first published *Why Should the Boss Listen to You?: The Seven Disciplines of the Trusted Strategic Advisor*, it quickly became a must-read for any who aspired to help leaders. It has continued to be so.

I have had dozens of clients—major American and international companies—that have embraced the book—and in particular the Three-Minute Drill advice-giving technique—in their own professional development programs. Its principles are timeless and yet, today, more timely than ever.

When Jim asked me to help him refresh the book, I was both honored and humbled. It's a mighty fine book all by itself. It doesn't need me or my insights to keep it a must-read. So my approach has been to be mostly in the background, refreshing things here and there, occasionally offering my own examples of things, and sometimes even elaborating on how over the years I've taken what I learned from Jim and built on it. But I wanted to preserve the essential Jim-ness that the first edition possesses. My role is more that of a Greek chorus, calling attention to key points, and offering new examples. That's why the author line is Jim with me, rather than Jim and me. This is his book. I'm honored to have played a small part in keeping it fresh.

The encyclopedia of crisis management: Visit Jim's website, www.e911.com, where hundreds of articles reside on various important topics related to Jim's and Fred's practices, managing urgent, crisis situations, and leadership problems. You can easily find the site map there that details each of the various items on the site itself.

During his 40-year career, Jim worked for more than 300 corporations, businesses, and government agencies. To help get a sense of the scope of his practice there are several indexes by topic and by type of organization and assignment topics.

The reader is urged to contact the authors for additional information on the various assignments and projects referred to. James E. Lukaszewski can be reached at jel@e911.com or 203-948-7029 and Helio Fred Garcia can be reached at www.logosconsulting.net; hfgarcia@logosconsulting.net, or 646-283-4000.

Acknowledgments

Jim's Acknowledgments:

In my acknowledgments for the original edition of *Why Should the Boss Listen to You?* I expressed gratitude to more than 25 people who had some role in conceiving, reviewing, and improving that book. Nearly 20 years later that gratitude is even greater, given the book's success. I renew that expression of gratitude to all who were there at the beginning, and who continue to inspire me.

Some of those also played a meaningful role in conceiving, reviewing, and improving this updated edition, now titled *Influencing Leaders*. I am particularly grateful to my sons, James Alexander and Charles Lukaszewski, for their persistent help and advice, especially in bringing this new book from idea to reality.

My Associate Kerrigan West came to us right out of college in 2002 in New York. She was one of our star Assistants for eight years. Under Barbara Lukaszewski she learned our business from the ground up. She served both Barbara and me with amazing skill. In 2010 Barbara and I moved the business back to Minneapolis. The only job loss was Kerrigan's. We did ask her to move to Minneapolis. She looked up, smiled, and said, "Barbara and Jim, there is only one thing I can't do for you . . . move to Minneapolis." She got a nice severance check. We all laughed.

In 2025 I moved back to New York to be near my grandchildren. Kerrigan has returned to work for me, now as my Associate, running my various projects and being enormously helpful with this book. She was trained by Barbara.

The most important acknowledgment belongs to Barbara Lukaszewski, my sunshine girl, the happiest person of my whole life. Wife, helper, pal, buddy, mother of our children, lover, business partner, editor, publisher, personal promoter, for 60 years. We met in high school in 1960. She was a sophomore. I had just graduated. It was a blind date starting in the afternoon at the General Ulysees Grant fountain in Chicago's Grant Park. She emerged from the shade into the afternoon sun, a beautiful blond vision in a white and yellow gingham dress. I was smitten.

Almost from the beginning she became devoted to me and I to her. We married in 1964, sons Chuck and James came in 1967 and 1968. She was a dental hygienist until she came to work for me in 1978. We worked together side by side until she passed away in 2019.

She ran our businesses, helped build my public relations practice, edited, published, and promoted my first 10 books, and worked with the publishers of the next 5. Constantly cheerful and truly happy. When she was around, you had to be happy too. She taught me what true happiness is.

Our devotion to each other was so obvious that those who came to know us were always asking, "How can you be so happy, you work together day and night, when you are apart you talk about getting together as soon as possible." Ours was truly a magical life. All day every day she worked to make me successful. She was a beautiful perfectionist. If you worked for her, you became a perfectionist, too—grammar, spelling, proofreading, constructing beautiful documents, all in real time, and you enjoyed learning from her.

As a one-person shop most of my career, we often competed against the biggest of the biggest for the toughest of the tough assignments. Our amazing record of success was because we had a policy of responding to all questions and inquiries within 24 hours, no matter what. The bigger the competition the longer it took for them to find who was available to put a committee together to explore what was being requested. We were almost always first.

She remembered everyone's name. If you happened to mention your great Aunt Alma's sore left knee, the next time you called us two years later, the first thing Barbara asked you was if Aunt Alma's knee was improving.

Our goal was response speed and responsiveness. When the phone rang, Barbara would greet and ask a few key questions. While the caller was briefly on hold waiting for me, Barbara would alert me but quickly fax or email crib sheets to the caller with likely tips for getting their response immediately under way, or several questions they were about to be asked by me.

Our philosophy was speed beats smart every time. The big guys, though very competent, always took time even to select who should or could respond. But most importantly as soon as we had a sense of the caller's problem, we immediately provided valuable advice whether we were hired or not. If it was a genuine crisis, there were victims who needed assistance and immediate response.

Throughout her life Barbara was generous and thoughtful. When our oldest granddaughter, Molly, was born Barbara wrote her a 10-page single-spaced letter recounting the history of our family and hers. Barbara sent the letter to our daughter-in-law Meri for safe keeping until Molly's 18th birthday. We were there when Molly opened it. What a beautiful surprise. That was when I learned of and got to read the letter too.

Barbara spent a portion of every day thinking of ways to make people happy, generally beginning with me. She retired, survived bilateral ovarian cancer, but succumbed to Alzheimer's. When I checked her into hospice care, the nurse asked me for her meds list. I responded that she didn't have one. The nurse then growled at me, "Everyone here has a meds list!" I mentioned that Barbara had a bottle of Tylenol and Ibuprofen in her suitcase.

Barbara was also little miss perfect, too. She really was. She made my life as perfect as it could possibly be. During her last three years she couldn't speak. She did manage to have an eight-word vocabulary: "I love you, Yes, No, Hi!, Real Good!" when she got a chocolate dessert. Sunshine girl to the end.

I also want to express gratitude to those who worked specifically to make this book a reality. First, Sarah Henson, President and Chief Legal Consultant at Anchor & Quill Consulting, who managed the long process of finalizing the contract with the publisher. And the team at Wiley, starting with Associate Publisher Jeanenne Ray, who chose to greenlight this new edition; Raven Buckler, Editorial Assistant, who managed the details; Michelle Hacker, Senior Managing Editor, who took the book from manuscript to publication; and Julie Kerr, the Development Editor who helped us fine-tune the manuscript.

Katie Garcia, Senior Advisor at Logos Consulting Group, and Sam Allington, Associate at Logos Consulting Group, reviewed the original *Why Should the Boss Listen to You?* and suggested ways to update and improve it for a new edition, and provided both counsel and logistical support, mostly to Fred, along the way.

Fred's Acknowledgments:

Nearly 20 years ago Jim asked me to read a manuscript he had just completed, and invited me, if I so desired, to endorse *Why Should the Boss Listen to You?* I read it and then endorsed it enthusiastically. In that endorsement, both in the book and on Amazon, I said, "Jim Lukaszewski is a master at both giving advice to leaders and coaching others to become trusted advisors. This book provides valuable tools and techniques to help enhance anyone's advisory skills, and to help earn the trust and confidence of those at the top."

Since then, I have used the book in my professional practice and in my teaching and have recommended it to clients and to other professors. So I begin by thanking Jim for including me on this journey from the beginning of this book. And especially for entrusting me in helping him to refresh, update, expand, and otherwise bring to life this new version, *Influencing Leaders*.

All of my writing projects, including this one, have benefitted from input from Katie Garcia, Logos Consulting Group Senior Advisor and Chief of Staff. She is also my daughter, and quite gifted at toggling between those two roles to keep me accountable as a colleague, as a writer and teacher, and as a person. I also thank Logos Consulting Group Associate Sam Allington, who helped especially in the early phases to document the content of the original book, and to identify areas for updates and improvement.

As in all of my work, I could not do what I do without the love and support of Laurel Colvin, the love of my life, and of our other daughter, Juliana Bronken.

Finally, I thank the hundreds of clients and thousands of students who have entrusted me to share Jim's wisdom, insights, and methods, and who then deployed them in the world, both validating the work itself and inspiring us to keep going.

About the Authors

James E. Lukaszewski (loo-ka-SHEV-skee) is America's Crisis Guru®. Jim has been a trusted strategic advisor for most of his career, both during his service in government and later as he became a communications management consultant. He is an internationally recognized speaker on crisis management, employee communications, ethics, media relations, public affairs, reputation preservation and restoration, and leadership.

Jim advises, coaches, and counsels the men and women who run very large corporations and organizations. His work as founder, CEO, and chairman of the Lukaszewski Group, Inc., is managing and counteracting tough, touchy, sensitive corporate communications issues. His broad-based experience ranges from media-initiated investigations to product recalls and plant closings, from criminal litigation to takeovers. The situations he helps resolve often involve conflict, controversy, community action, activist opposition, and civil or criminal litigation. Jim has the unique ability to help executives look at problems from a variety of principled perspectives. He has personally counseled, coached, and guided thousands of executives in organizations large and small from many cultures. He is one of the few who can and truly does coach CEOs.

In addition to *Why Should the Boss Listen to You?: The Seven Disciplines of the Trusted Strategic Advisor*, Jim has also authored 13 other books, including:

- *Influencing Public Attitudes: Strategies That Reduce the Media's Power*, 1992, which remains a classic work in the field of direct communication.

- *Executive Action Crisis Communication Management System: War Stories and Crisis Communication Strategies*, 2005, an anthology.
- *Crisis Communication Planning Strategies, a Workbook; Crisis Communication Plan Components and Models: Crisis Communication Management Readiness; and Media Relations During Emergencies*, 2005.
- *Lukaszewski on Crisis Communication: What Your CEO Needs to Know About Reputation Risk and Crisis Management*, 2103, edited by Kristen Noakes-Fry.
- *The Manager's Guide to Handling the Media in Crisis: Saying & Doing the Right Thing When It Matters Most*, 2016, edited by Kristen Noakes-Fry.
- *The Decency Code: The Leader's Path to Building Integrity and Trust*, 2020 co-authored with Steven Harrison.

Jim has published dozens of monographs and hundreds of articles on critical communication subjects.

Jim served on the New York University faculty for 22 years.

Jim has received the highest awards from organizations of professional communication, including (partial list):

- ➢ 2024 – The Platinum Award PRSA Midwest District.
- ➢ 2020 – Lifetime Achievement Awards by Trust Across America—Trust Around the World™.
- ➢ 2019 – Trust Across America Top Thought Leaders and Trust.
- ➢ 2017 – Outstanding Leadership Award, The Logos Institute for Crisis Management and Executive Leadership.
- ➢ May 2015 – IABC Fellow, International Association of Business Communicators.
- ➢ 2013 and 2014 – Donald G. Padilla Distinguished Practitioner Award, Minnesota PRSA.
- ➢ 2013 and 2014 – Top 100 Thought Leader in Trustworthy Business, Trust Across America.
- ➢ 2013 – Soundview's Best New Business Book, *Lukaszewski on Crisis Communication*.

- ➢ 2010 – Public Relations Society of America (PRSA), John W. Hill Award for Lifetime Achievement.
- ➢ 2007 – Mercury Award, PRSA Greater Connecticut Chapter.
- ➢ 2006 – Lloyd B. Dennis Distinguished Leadership Award, PRSA.
- ➢ 2005 – Lifetime Achievement Award, PR News.
- ➢ 2005 – Patrick Jackson Award for Distinguished Service, PRSA.

Helio (Él-yoo) Fred Garcia is a coach, counselor, teacher, writer, and speaker whose clients include some of the largest and best-known companies and organizations in the world. For more than 45 years Fred has helped leaders build trust, inspire loyalty, and lead effectively. He has worked in dozens of countries on six continents.

Fred is the president of the crisis management firm Logos Consulting Group and executive director of the Logos Institute for Crisis Management and Executive Leadership.

Fred has been on the New York University faculty since 1988. He is an adjunct professor of management in NYU's Stern School of Business. He teaches crisis management in the Executive MBA program, where he was named 2016 Executive MBA Great Professor. Through his Stern appointment he also teaches crisis management in the TRIUM Global Executive MBA program, a consortium of NYU Stern, London School of Economics and Political Science, and HEC Management Paris. He is an adjunct associate professor of management and communication in NYU's School of Professional Studies, MS in Public Relations and Corporate Communication program, where he has twice received the Dean's award for teaching excellence. In that program he teaches courses in communication strategy; communication ethics, law, and regulation; and crisis communication.

Fred is also an adjunct professor at Columbia University's School of Engineering and Applied Sciences, Professional Development and Leadership program. He teaches leadership communication, ethics, and crisis to BS, MS, and PhD engineering and applied science students. Since 1990 he has been a contract lecturer on crisis and leadership communication at Wharton/UPenn. He has guest lectured at dozens of universities on four continents.

For eight years Fred was a member of leadership faculty in the Master in Advanced Studies in Security Policy and Crisis Management of the Swiss Federal Institute of Technology (ETH) Zurich. In 2011 he was an

International Distinguished Scholar at Tsinghua University in Beijing. For 35 years he has taught in schools and commands of the U.S. military. He received the U.S. Army War College Certificate in Leader Development—National Security and Strategy.

Fred is a highly sought keynote and motivational speaker. He has keynoted major conferences and events on five continents. Fred speaks about leadership communication; crisis management; business, science, and communication ethics; disinformation; journalist/source relationships; and ways to maintain trust in difficult situations. Fred is a member of the Forbes Coaches Council.

Fred has received the Public Relations Society of America—New York awards for mentoring; for lifetime achievement; and the President's Award for "the highest standards of ethical conduct and outstanding service within the public relations profession."

Fred is the author of six prior books:

- *Reputation Management: The Key to Successful Public Relations and Corporate Communication*, co-author with John Doorley. Fifth Edition, 2025; Fourth Edition, 2020; Third Edition, 2015; Second Edition, 2010; First Edition, 2007; Korean Edition, 2016; Vietnamese Edition, 2021.
- *The Trump Contagion: How Incompetence, Dishonesty, and Neglect Led to the Worst-Handled Crisis in American History*, 2024.
- *Words on Fire: The Power of Incendiary Language and How to Confront It*, 2020.
- *The Agony of Decision: Mental Readiness and Leadership in a Crisis*, 2017. Named #2 of 50 Best Crisis Management Books of All Time by Book Authority, 2018. Chinese Edition, 2020.
- *The Power of Communication: Skills to Build Trust, Inspire Loyalty, and Lead Effectively*, 2012. Named to the U.S. Marine Corps Commandant's Professional Reading List, 2013-2018. Chinese Edition, 2014. Second Edition pending, 2026, with co-author Katie Garcia.
- *Crisis Communication,* two volumes, 1998.

Introduction: Leaders and Their Advisors

To be a trusted strategic adviser requires putting yourself in another person's shoes, looking at the world from their perspective, and letting that approach dominate how you think, how you speak, how you coach, and how you contribute.

It also means recognizing that an executive is rarely looking for advisor consensus or that single big idea, but rather good solid insight, options, and even conflicting views for their own decision-making. Executives execute based on the choices at hand especially when the clock is close to running out.

Professional Potholes

Some aspects of this work are so obvious that they often are overlooked and become professional potholes. The first is that every organization, whether it is for profit, not-for-profit, government, or military, can be divided into two parts: staff and operations. And, of course, operations is where the business is run. It is where the products are sold or manufactured, where the services are provided, that that sort of thing. Wherever the business or organization is generating revenue that is the operating side of the business.

Operators run the business organization; staff functions exist to help those operators do a better job, every day. The staff side of the business essentially comprises public relations, human resources, law, finance, security, government relations, IT, strategic planning, regulatory affairs, marketing, and other service functions. Staff functions are expenses against revenue. In other words, staff are always on the cost side of the business ledger.

Staff often spent a lot of time debating their bottom-line value. To most operating executives this line of thinking is a waste of time, although operators are often greatly amused by the lengths that staff will go to justify their ideas and even their existence. The more that staff tried to justify their existence based on their contribution to the bottom line, the more intensively the CEO and other senior operating executives subject staff expenses to scrutiny and measurability. If you are intent on basing your staff value case on your bottom-line contribution you are likely to be working alone and worrying a lot.

The premise behind being a trusted strategic advisor is that you bring extraordinary value to your relationship with executives, well beyond the cost impact of your advice. Most staff people make the mistake of assuming that if they are in the presence of senior leadership from time to time, they are automatically looked at as at least an occasional member of the inner circle. This is what we call the face-time fantasy. Actually, you know in your heart and in your gut that it's a fantasy. The boss may know the names of your grandchildren or your kids, where you vacation, where your wife or husband was born, where you went to school, or your golf score. But almost none of this has anything to do with running the business. Your job as we will learn in this book is to make certain that the time you spend with executives is limited, focused, and overwhelmingly in their operational interest.

We will delve more deeply into the discipline sections. Right from the beginning take a breath and lose that self-imposed false impression that the more time you get to spend with the boss in a variety of settings, the more likely it is that they will turn to you for advice.

Five Imperatives for the Trusted Strategic Advisor

Any staff person—or any consultant—needs to do five things to become a trusted advisor to senior leaders:

1. Jettison staff-based assumptions.
2. See the whole board.
3. Tolerate strategic ambiguity but strive for certainty.
4. Maximize your prerogatives.
5. Develop real expertise beyond your staff functions.

Let us examine each of these imperatives.

Jettison Staff-Based Assumptions

One of the most profound underlying concepts in this book is designed to convey to you the imperative to set aside all your staff-based assumptions and to orient your life, your thinking, and your recommendations to the perspectives, viewpoints, and issues of those you advise.

Failure to do this effectively will relegate you to being "just a PR guy," "just an HR person," "just a bean counter," "just a cop without a gun or badge." Leaving your staff assumptions behind is among the hardest disciplines of the trusted advisor. You will be working from a much broader perspective, first and always defined by the issues and questions facing those you counsel.

Although this reality was obvious to each of us from the early days of our career, it came to Jim most powerfully following a speech he gave in 1991 to the International Security Management Association in Florida. He was talking about his favorite subject, crisis management, to more than 100 of the nation's most senior corporate security offers officers. The presentation and workshop lasted for nearly three hours. By the time it was finished and Jim had answered all the questions, he was late getting to the airport. As he checked in with his office within the 45 minutes following the presentation, he had already received about half a dozen messages from participants. Although, of course, Jim liked to think that his presentations are powerful, important, and helpful, this was unusual. Once back in his office he began returning the calls. It was clear that he had said something important during the presentation, but he was having difficulty figuring out what it was. So he began asking each participant who called, "What did I say that struck a nerve with everyone? My phone has been ringing off the hook."

The senior vice president for security of a Fortune 50 company replied, "It's easy. We were all buzzing about the comment you made that all the problems in organizations are management problems before they are any other kind of problem. You were talking about the fact that if you want to successfully prepare management to deal with problems, you need to go to the CEO first, get their buy-in (through understanding what worries the CEO most). From there, you made the point that doing lots of preparation work and presenting a finished plan and process to management largely developed by outsiders—or even by insiders—will probably be rejected by top managers and the boss, if not out of hand, certainly when problems occur, the worst possible time period. I thought I could hear a hundred light bulbs go on in the audience at the same time when you finished this portion of your presentation." He said the calls were about helping these individuals, already the very senior staffers, get the boss's ear for that all important first conversation.

Each staff function tends to apply its staff disciplines to every problem it sees. Communicators look at everything as a communication problem; finance as a finance problem; HR as a people problem; security as a problem of risk—you get the idea.

The principal reason staff people are excluded from operating meetings is that they bring too tight a staff focus. Most leaders, managers, or even supervisors believe that they are good communicators, financially savvy, and aware of their surroundings. They assume that they know the risks they face, and can add, subtract, multiply, and divide. From the start you are facing an environment that is not exactly staff friendly. This is a powerful insight. Dump the tendency to see everything through the lens of your staff experience. Yes, your perspective does matter, provided that *first*, it reflects the attitudes and needs of the managers you are advising.

Let us put this into even sharper focus. One of the more frequent questions Jim gets is this: "How do I convince my boss to change something because big mistakes are being made, but the boss will not listen to me? If a couple of things I suggested are implemented the boss will be much more successful in accomplishing their goals." Jim's response to that staff person is, "Why are you pushing this so hard? Obviously, the boss does not want to take your suggestion. Unless what the boss is doing is immoral, illegal, completely stupid, or financially irresponsible, the boss is the boss for a reason. It is the boss's career and the boss's decision to make. Move on to something else. If what the boss is doing is immoral, illegal, irresponsible, or something along those lines, you have to address a professional employment decision." The message is this: remember who is driving the bus and whose bus it is.

If you have a problem with this perspective, we suggest that you put this book back on the shelf and look for something else to read.

See the Whole Board

If you have been tutored by or have taken classes from a skilled chess player, you know that one of the most important lessons is to keep the entire board in mind. You have to look at the whole board constantly as you plan and make your moves, assessing, analyzing, and forecasting the other moves that could result. As you have probably observed, some people are so skilled at this that they can actually analyze the board and predict how many moves are required to finish the game. Being a trusted advisor is very much like this concept of seeing the whole board.

Another way to think of seeing the whole board is to recognize the power of patterns. There is a discussion in much greater depth than Chapter 8 about pattern recognition as one of the seven disciplines. But at this point it is important to recognize that many things in relationships, business, politics, and human endeavors fit patterns of past events, in other venues or perhaps even in your own. Understanding the patterns of human behavior, the patterns of thinking, the patterns of events, the patterns of leadership, and the collateral issues these events trigger is another way to bring insight and understanding to leaders in ways far different from those they can achieve by themselves.

Your job as the trusted advisor is to look over the entire field of interest—the barriers, threats, constraints, options, and opportunities—and keep them in mind as you provide advice and recommendations to those you coach and counsel. You are consciously building the discipline of maintaining distance and altitude from everything that you talk about and recommend. Dispassion is a significant ingredient in establishing management trust, respect, and credibility in those with senior-level responsibilities. They need to feel that your advice comes with reliable objectivity, experience, and insight.

One metaphor to keep in mind here is always to operate at 50,000 feet. Altitude changes attitudes. Altitude gives you an important perspective on every aspect of those areas that are in sight. It also brings dispassion and fosters objectivity. Some of the greatest insights you will have as a trusted strategic adviser are those driven by your ability to see a larger view, the more strategic view. As you will see in Chapter 1, the leader's principal assignment is to look over the horizon and see what is there. When you too can observe from a significant altitude, you can see over the horizon to explore the environment that surrounds where the leader is looking and, perhaps, even beyond where the leader is looking. It is essential to maintain this sense of perspective.

Tolerate Strategic Ambiguity, but Strive for Certainty

Consultants and advisors are fundamentally option-and-alternative-finders rather than solution-finders. This is because leaders recognize that having a solution is oftentimes the least of their worries. What really matters is finding a process to get something that works, almost anything that works. This is another area where the trusted advisor plays a crucial role.

Sometimes your role with a leader will be ambiguous, often because the leader's behavior is ambiguous. You do need to have a methodology for seeking clarification and for generating clarity. The more important point is that a leader's life is ambiguous and difficult. Solutions and answers seem easy for consultants, so it can be frustrating, irritating, and sometimes even embarrassing when leaders fail to grasp or intentionally ignore what is excellent, even achievable, advice. Develop a tolerance for what leaders instinctively know will keep them successful. The leader's ability to manage and turn strategies into processes will lengthen the time required to achieve results but ultimately will productively move the organization. Resist the common advisor frustration of getting the process part done.

Maximize Your Prerogatives

Being influential means having power. Getting things to happen today, when you want to or need to, is about creating immediate, visible impact through actions or decisions by the boss. You can also choose to be influential over longer time frames—whichever strategy best fits the objective you seek to achieve. A longer-term approach may mean less immediate impact. Some bosses are more comfortable with this style of counselling because they permit only limited visibility and credit-sharing when workable ideas and decision options come from the suggestions of others. The ongoing clash of egos and ideas at the top often submerges the authorship of ideas. The benefit of this approach is that things that come out of top management are in the category of "being invented here." Although this can be frustrating for the advisor, this is the reality of working and advising at this altitude. The boss always gets the credit.

Actually, seeing your recommendations become marching orders in real time is something amazing to behold and to achieve. Having impact tends to mean that the executive being advised or the group being counseled "does what you tell them."

The satisfaction of having immediate impact is often a central motivation for becoming a trusted strategic adviser. Leaders at every level constantly need special thinking, advice, commentary, and analysis in the achievement-focused environment that is today's "high performance" organization. There is the added reality that whatever recommendation must be doable using methods and approaches that operations can directly implement and must produce constructive results promptly. The issue for the trusted strategic adviser is that their advice is always modified, adapted, and frequently used in fragments, with someone else taking or getting the credit.

It helps to be realistic about what leaders in their organizations can actually accomplish in a short period of time. Achieving operational impact can be difficult because the staff person is focused too far away from operations. The resulting lack of knowledge inhibits their ability to make powerful recommendations. This situation is buffered by the knowledge that many breakthrough ideas and solutions are extremely simple in nature and require only limited influence rather than an in-depth knowledge of operations or even finance.

If you are a more junior staffer, there is the nagging question, "If I'm several levels down from the big boss, how can I get my ideas seen at the top of the organization?" The correct answer has always been to work through your current boss and your current boss's boss. Sooner or later they will get tired of listening to you and will instead send you to make your own case. Or they could fire you. In either case a promotion, enhanced personal responsibility, or a constructive change in your career is likely. Successful advisors are self-selected, self-appointed, self-energizing, self-evaluating, and relentlessly persistent.

Teach your boss what and how to teach their boss. If there is no chance of this working, there is virtually no chance you're getting information to the top. That means it may be time to look elsewhere for a position where your talents, knowledge, skills, and abilities can be greater appreciated, or to grow in an entirely different direction—whether within your own organization or, perhaps, somewhere else.

Develop Real Expertise Beyond Your Staff Function

If you want to receive access to operating executives beyond routine staff consultations, you must possess, perhaps above all else, some real, recognizable expertise. This expertise generally needs to move beyond your area of staff knowledge. The reasoning is that most senior operators feel fairly confident of their knowledge base in your area. They assume that your competence in that area comes with the territory. If you stay within the box of your staff expertise, you will be called only when the boss thinks that staff expertise is required, usually to validate something they already want to do in your area, and you will be told what to do and when to do it, what to say and when to say it.

Opportunities abound for providing special expertise both from a staff perspective and operationally. In Chapter 1, where we talk specifically about understanding bosses and boards of directors, you will learn about those special advisors who meet on a nearly daily basis about the organization they lead. You will learn about the kinds of information they seek continuously, and it may be that you can develop expertise and gather this information for the boss or other relevant senior officials. Once you have identified this special expertise and act to develop it, you will also need to develop a strategy to make certain that these skills, areas of knowledge, or abilities are available to senior leadership; we will talk about this topic in Chapter 10.

Look around at those in the inner circle, those whom the bosses consult routinely, and ask yourself why these people are more sought after than you or your colleagues. One of the crucial reasons is they bring this sense of real expertise to the boss's territory. If you cannot figure out why someone is in the inner circle, ask the boss why. The answer will either be very enlightening or totally underwhelming, but ask.

It Takes a Disciplined Approach

The lion's share of this book is about you and about how you will need to change yourself to be more successful as a trusted advisor.

The chapters in Part II discuss each of the seven disciplines you will need to develop, refine, or strengthen:

1. **Be Trustworthy.** Earn the respect and confidence of those you advise.
2. **Become a Verbal Visionary.** Recognize that giving advice is an art and a skill that primarily depends on your verbal accomplishment.
3. **Develop a Management Perspective.** Look at the world through the leaders' eyes.
4. **Think Strategically.** This is perhaps the most valued quality of senior advisors—looking for methods and models to achieve different, novel, often unique solutions.
5. **Understand the Power of Patterns.** Examine similar events to extract lessons for the future; the ability to understand patterns is sometimes referred to as the source of wisdom about what is going to happen.
6. **Advise Constructively.** Provide advice using a structure, format, and context that can be easily absorbed and acted on by those you advise.
7. **Show the Boss How to Use Your Advice.** Showing the manager or boss how to put your advice into practice is essential. Most bosses learn how to work with advisors through trial and error. The best advisors always help their clients understand how to use the advice they received from many different quarters.

Are You Ready?

One purpose of this introduction to the book is to help you assess whether or not you really have what it takes to achieve the role of trusted strategic advisor. In the assessment that follows, you will ask yourself some very serious questions to determine just how committed you are to becoming a trusted strategic advisor or to see how far along you may already be.

Assessment: Are You Ready to Be a Trusted Advisor?

- Do I have the stomach for the intense, conflict ridden, and often confrontational environment in which decisions are made at the senior levels of organizations?
- Can I dispassionately assess the strengths, weaknesses, opportunities, options, and threats of the organization from a variety of useful perspectives?
- What is the real expertise, behind my area of staff knowledge, that I bring to those who run my organization?
- Will I commit to mastering the seven disciplines and harness their power for my success and that of those I advise?
- How do I answer the question, "Why should the boss listen to me?"

PART I

The Realities of Advising Top Executives

1 How Leaders Think and Operate: The Pressures, What Matters, the Obstacles, and the Solutions

Chapter Outline

- Pressures Leaders Are Under
  - Leaders Are Having a Lot Less Fun
  - The Limits of Leadership
  - The Loneliness of Leadership
- What Leaders Do
  - Leadership Is About Tomorrow
  - Making It Up as We Go
  - Daily Intrusions
- Why Leaders Fail
  1. Failure to Deliver on What Was Promised or Expected When They Got the Job
  2. Over-Optimism
  3. People Problems
  4. Distractions
  5. Stuck in the Mud
- How Leaders Achieve Success
  1. Focus
  2. Limit the Number of Objectives to Be Achieved
  3. Build Support and Create Followers
  4. Fix What Is Broken Fast
  5. Finish What You Start
  6. Start to Stop What's Not Working or Not Going to Succeed
- Implications and Applications for the Advisor
- Question for You to Consider

How the day-to-day world of leaders applies to you, how leaders make decisions, five reasons leaders fail, and six behaviors for leadership success.

The place to begin our discussion on achieving the status of a Trusted Strategic Advisor is, of course, talking about the world of leaders and how they operate.

The nature of leadership has changed in many important ways in the last few decades. Whether a leader is the CEO of a multinational company, a tech start-up, a large local utility, a taxi company, a dairy, or even the superintendent of the school district, gaining these positions used to represent the pinnacle achievement of one's lifetime. There are many powerful realities that drive the world of today's CEO, as we will see in this chapter. Becoming a Trusted Strategic Advisor requires a clear sense of these realities and of the role that CEOs play.

Pressures Leaders Are Under

Look at the CEO's world. It is very, very different than most people imagine: All training for CEOs is on the job.

There really is no school for becoming a CEO.

Talk to those who have other high-level jobs, and many do before they become CEOs. Talk to Chief Operating Officers, watching from next door, second-guessing their bosses, certain they could run the place better. Yet, the moment the top job becomes theirs, the new incumbent instantly realizes that the job is completely different from anything that could possibly have imagined.

The new CEO also notices that they are alone. There is only one CEO in the organization.

Every single day for a CEO is a new learning experience because there is no manual and no one to train them. Surprisingly, the CEO discovers, too, just how limited the freedom to act really is. Wait a minute, you say, the CEO is the boss; they can do anything. The reality is very different. Being a 21st-century CEO is extraordinarily stressful.

Leaders Are Having a Lot Less Fun

A brief tour of the reality of today's executive leadership world will reinforce the fact that these jobs are extremely difficult, challenging, and frustrating.

The average tenure of corporate leaders is declining, as is the average tenure of their key staff. There are two reasons for this, one global, one local. As larger organizations globalize, one of the most significant features of global corporations is the youth of their leadership. According to Bloomberg in early 2023, the age of newly appointed CEOs peaked at 56 in 2021, with quite a few new CEOs over 60. But starting in 2022, the average age of new CEOs fell to 54, with nearly 30% under 50. One S&P 500 CEO was 42.[1]

The second reason is that people in general know a lot more at a significantly younger age than they used to. The amount of knowledge a 35-year-old can bring to the business in the modern era is perhaps two to three times what it was just 25 years ago. These younger managers are indeed capable of leading large business organizations.

CEO turnover dropped during the COVID-19 pandemic, as many companies felt the need for stability and familiarity to get through the crisis. CEO turnover dropped from 11.6% in 2020 to 9.6% in 2021 among Russell 3000 companies. Job turnover hit record highs during the pandemic but not among CEOs. A 2022 article states that CEO turnover began to rise again. Within 2021, there wasn't a single instance of forced exit among Russell 3000 companies.[2]

Another important factor is the succession failure factor. According to Dan Ciampa, former CEO and now counselor and coach to many CEOs and boards of directors, who is a recognized authority on CEO succession, one-third to one-half of new chief executives fail within the first 18 months. Some of these flame-outs can be attributed to poor strategic choices by the new leader. Some result when the board makes an imperfect choice or overestimates a candidate's abilities and potential, hiring a leader whose skill set doesn't fit the context. Sometimes the new leader is obviously responsible for the problems created, other times the board is rightly blamed.[3]

A close look shows that it is rarely that simple. When the succession fails, responsibilities are almost always shared.

Fewer than half of involuntarily retired executives regain a comparable position in their lifetime. More and more management literature is being devoted to these individuals and their inability to recover following sudden, unplanned separation from their top jobs.

Non-operational issues, for example, globalization, adverse legislation, and anti-corporate activism, are intruding with greater regularity. These interruptions are soft, highly emotional, and require an entirely different attitude by management. The Sarbanes-Oxley legislation, enacted by the United States Congress in 2002, introduced a distinctly moral focus into daily operations, an approach that continues to antagonize and irritate many business leaders. This moral focus is frustrating for staff functions to discuss, decode, and decipher. The Sarbanes-Oxley law forced integrity and compliance concerns forward, basically through threat of criminal prosecution. This legislation has gotten management's attention, at every level, but especially at the top, where the greatest risk now rests.

One of the major impacts in this moral focus on leadership is the extraordinary expansion of compliance activities and requirements in many companies combined with often very intricate codes of conduct. They are very intensive and ongoing activities as managements attempt to clarify what specific behaviors are required as well as specific behaviors that are prohibited. The Trusted Strategic Advisor is deeply engaged in these now operationalized Human Resource activities and often business mandates. The role of a Trusted Strategic Advisor includes helping new CEOs orchestrate their first 100–300 days in office.

Another facet of the non-operational issue for large local and national companies, but especially for the global company, is the rise in power and influence of non-government organizations (NGOs). This has introduced a whole new level of stresses, strains, and potentially negative visibilities for business organizations.

In large organizations, globalization increasingly requires staff functions to work together across intellectual, international, and intercultural lines, and around the clock. It is definitely becoming more complicated to be a senior staff advisor in large organizations. The demands on the leader have increased significantly. On the one hand, they are asked to do more, faster, while on the other they are forced to reduce staff support as an indicator of their ability to be successful.

With all these distractions, coaching and counseling leaders require important fundamental shifts in mindset. The trusted advisor needs to realize that the CEO, while still captain of the ship, is operating under increasingly complicated navigation rules and pressures.

The Limits of Leadership

Deciding on a course of action is one thing, but getting the organization ready, willing, and able to move in that direction is an entirely different task and challenge. Successful leaders and their advisors learn to recognize the limits of CEO effectiveness.

One of the first large companies Jim worked for retained him to develop a marketing strategy for one of its highly technical product divisions, which was beginning to plateau as more competition entered the field. Jim and another person spent significant time developing several unique approaches for the organization to consider. When they made their presentation to senior management, it was enthusiastically received. The senior managers were engaged in conversations, asked questions, actually remarked at how sensible and important all of the ideas they presented seemed to be. It was one of the best presentations Jim can recall making in all the years he has been a consultant.

They all went to lunch together, and Jim sat next to the CEO. He seemed quite pleased. So Jim asked him, "With the reception this morning, how much of what we proposed is likely to be initiated?" Without hesitating, the CEO said, "I'd guess about four or five percent."

Jim was absolutely stunned. In fact, he had that sinking feeling in his stomach; you know the one where you have made a great mistake. After a brief hesitation, he asked, "Did I make a mistake? Did I misunderstand what happened this morning?" The CEO's answer was again quick and profound. He said, "Look, I'm just the CEO here. This place is run by the 7,500 employees who show up to work every day. What they will want to do and can do will determine the direction we're going. I'm 57 years old; if I stay healthy, I'll probably be CEO here for another seven to eight years. Absent some catastrophe such as tremendous business loss, stock drop, or takeover, if I can move this organization five to seven degrees in new directions every year, I will have made a substantial contribution during my brief term as leader. We're kind of like an aircraft carrier," he said. "Once we move in a direction, it takes a lot of energy to change that direction. Of course, torpedoes, hurricanes, or collisions can make a big difference, if they come along."

Leaders recognize and work to maintain the momentum of their organization and what it takes to change, reshape, and perfect that momentum.

Leader aspirations and behaviors often create an exuberance among staff functions that overestimates situations and is overly optimistic about results and about what can be changed. The leader's immediate staff often seems eager to simply move key organizational components or ideas around according to some checklist or set of theoretical ideas, based on what they assume the boss wants. The lesson of the CEO's 5 to 7% is that the greatest successes are often, at first, underwhelming. While much is desired, far less can actually be achieved; yet meaningful progress will still be made.

The Loneliness of Leadership

Leaders are often lonely. The concept of leadership loneliness will echo throughout the pages of this book. Several predictable consequences occur as an individual is elevated within an organization.

First, the sense of isolation and loneliness tends to increase because fewer people are privy to information at higher levels. Mitigating this isolation of leadership is one of the key roles for the trusted advisor.

Second, a filtration and sanitizing process occurs as information is passed up to the top. Most corporate advisory boards and boards of directors include a significant percentage of CEOs as peers to senior leaders. This facilitates the sharing of experiences between those who have similar relevant life and work histories. The presence of these senior peers often compensates for the lack of information that CEOs generally have as they make decisions about the futures of their organizations. The late Jack Welch, being interviewed on public television shortly after he had retired from his chairmanship at General Electric, was asked by an interviewer, "What was the worst part about being chairman of this huge U.S. corporation?" Welch answered without a second's hesitation, "Being the last to know."[4] This circumstance does tend to be a great frustration to those who lead.

Third, the higher the altitude, the thinner the leader's skin. Increasing seniority often comes with decreasing tolerance for questions, questioners, those who push back, and people with negative approaches. This can be a fatal flaw in management leadership. It is a major cause for isolation at the top and a powerful barrier to knowing what really is happening at various levels in the organizations.

Fourth, as managers advance and become senior managers and leaders, the "yes, sir/ma'am" mentality that pervades these high-level environments leads to an exaggerated sense of their own abilities: They believe that they are good communicators, financially savvy, and aware of their surroundings and the risks they face. They have enough mathematical competence to get along. Absent sensible and meaningful evaluation, what else are they to believe?

In this environment, at this altitude, it is a principal role of the Trusted Strategic Advisor to recognize these four circumstances and to constantly, relentlessly, and endlessly work against these patterns.

What Leaders Do

The CEO has two powerful assignments in any organization. The first job is to look to the future; that is, go over the horizon to see what is out there and then come back and tell the organization a bit about where it is headed, perhaps, what some of the pitfalls might be and, most importantly, what some of the deadlines are.

The second principal task of the CEO is to find the people-power required to achieve the organization's mission. Unlike the manager, whose job is to achieve objectives, complete programs, and work inside of the box, the leader's role is to work almost exclusively outside of the box in this energizing arena of strategy, future accomplishment, and managing the destiny of the organization.

The big decision work of executives, that is, those who execute at the top of the organization, is pretty much done by the time the operating budgets are in place, the program established, and a course for progress is being set. This is because, of course, others do the implementation. The leader's job shifts to observation, education, course correction, evaluation, inspiration, and motivation.

In Fred's executive coaching practice he has noted a pattern: The higher a leader goes in an organization, the less success and failure is driven by technical competence and the more it is driven by communication: by the ability to inspire; to align people around a common purpose; to keep people energized. By the time one is at the very top, Fred has found, communication can take up to 80% of the leader's time. And a big part of that is repeating the same theme over time. Many leaders hate repeating themselves. But Fred admonishes then: One of the burdens of leadership is to have a very high tolerance for repetition.

Indeed, Jack Welch's successor at General Electric, Jeff Immelt, said frequently that every leader needs to constantly remind their people of the few most important things to the organization.[5]

Leadership success depends on leader-driven communication. In fact, personal communication, in good times and bad, is the most powerful tool leaders have.

When Jim examines how to move organizations, successful leader communicators follow a fairly interesting pattern of mostly verbal communication and participation with their employees, executives, and others (see Table 1.1).

The math is correct, even though unusual, because the job of a leader is a 24/7 proposition. Anyone who does anything on a 24/7 basis, by definition, can accomplish substantially more than any peer or non-leader working more regular hours.

As you can tell by this distribution of time, the CEO and senior leadership will be spending significant amounts of time explaining, coaching, interpreting, reiterating, and monitoring the progress of their strategies, plans, and outcomes. This is far different from the notion that these senior people are busy making big decisions every single day about things that can change the company's direction or the company's history. Even during enormously stressful times like mergers, acquisitions, takeovers, or divestitures, the actual number of major decisions executives make that matter is extremely small. It is the failure to communicate even these small decisions that is often the root cause of much bigger operational failures.

Table 1.1 Jim's Empirical Analysis of Top Leaders' Communication Activity

Decision-Making:	5%
Articulating:	40%
Coaching/Teaching/Motivating:	40%
Forecasting (Guessing):	5%
Admiration Building:	6%
Reputation Repair:	1%
Repeating, Re-emphasizing, Re-interpreting:	20%
Total:	117%

Recently Jim was interviewed by a top management team for a very large company that was heading into labor negotiations. The prospects were fairly gloomy. The board was concerned about conflicting approaches that had been suggested, and they wanted to hear Jim's. When Jim finished explaining his concept to them, their first reaction was, "Well Jim, from what you propose, we're going to spend a lot of time talking to employees." Jim's response was, "What else have you got to do that matters?" They laughed as they realized this was something of crucial importance and they really had to make the time to get it done.

Leadership Is About Tomorrow

Why is it that when the boss walks in the room, people's voices drop, everybody looks in that direction, and a sense of anticipation tends to build? It is because the only one in the room who knows where we are going, in other words, about tomorrow, is the leader or CEO who just walked in.

We all want to know where we will be tomorrow. In fact, whenever a boss or leader enters the room, the first obligation is to share some of the latest news that only the boss gets to know or would happen to have. This is, in fact, one of the most powerful reasons why being a Trusted Strategic Advisor is such an interesting position to hold.

You can only get that future view of where we are headed when standing next to and being around the person at the head of the line, the person who is making the decisions and choosing the future.

Leaders work in a future tense. The CEO is the chief strategist, and strategy is always about tomorrow's goals. This is because leadership is truly about tomorrow and what lies ahead. Contrast this with much of staff activity in your own experience. Some are busy defending yesterday and making excuses for things that have not yet happened, while still trying to leverage their way forward without the kind of forward-thinking and extraordinary insight leaders tend to expect.

Leaders avoid yesterday's thinking because it can be very confusing and unproductive. Besides, yesterday is already owned by everybody else from their own perspective. The past is owned by others intellectually, sometimes physically, perhaps financially, and certainly emotionally. And everyone's perception of yesterday is unique and almost always at odds with the perception of others, especially the victims. The fascination of leadership and leaders is that most of their work is in territory yet to be owned or occupied by anyone. This is the definition of tomorrow. It is an intellectual area where people can come together and where engineering solutions and ideas are still possible because tomorrow is where most people want to be in some positive, constructive way.

The Trusted Strategic Advisor constantly needs to decide whether to be a force for yesterday or a force for tomorrow. The closer you are in tune with tomorrow, the more likely your compatibility will be with the leader you are advising.

Making It Up as We Go

One of the greatest surprises about leaders is that much of what they do is more or less made up on the spot. Jim discovered this early in his career, when he had the chance to coach the CEO of a large insurance company in the Midwest. To coach at this level, you have to meet the person you will be coaching ahead of the scheduled session and there has to be almost an instant chemistry. It is about chemistry—can you work together; do you have this feeling that you are both on the same page?

Jim's "beauty contest" interview with this CEO took place in his wonderful, exotic office at the top of a very tall building. The view was amazing. The office had three full window walls; it was awesome. It was also really intimidating. As they began talking, it was pretty evident that the CEO had a "visitor management approach" because visitors asked the same questions about the view every time.

The moment a visitor starts to speak or ask questions, the CEO takes the visitor's arm, leads him or her first to window number one, then around the perimeter answering all the questions about each wall—pointing out landmarks, history, useful details—at about 45–60 seconds per window. As he began explaining the third window view, Jim's brain was screaming at him to, "Say something really important, real soon. Only one wall left, and that one has the door." Jim's mental voice commanded, "If you want to get this job you better ask an important question now."

So, Jim managed to interrupt the CEO with a question. "Tell me something, do you always know what to do?" he asked. "You run a company of

14,000 employees; I have a company of 14 employees. My people expect me to solve today's problems and move ahead for tomorrow, following a plan. Do you know what to do every minute?"

He looked at Jim, smiled, and said, "Don't you ever tell anybody this, but I think the board actually hired me because I had a good sense of where we would need to go, and at least half of my important decisions would be carried out by people who really knew what they were doing. They felt that I could estimate and make the right decisions in the grey areas at least 25 percent of the time. The remaining 25 percent they sort of left to me to find out for myself."

"But I'll tell you something," he continued, pointing at the door, "Every employee in this company thinks I have the answers. They think that I have a plan. I've got news for you, there is no plan. But if I were going to tell this to the people that work for me, they wouldn't believe it for a minute."

What Jim learned from that encounter, and it has been with him ever since, is the recognition that CEOs in particular are making it up 25 percent of the time. They have to create what is next. They are making it up based on their experience or lack of it, on their concerns or their fears, and oftentimes on the perceived opportunities as well. This is an extremely interesting insight to have. When Jim is in meetings, and the meetings are wandering off track, once in a while he will turn to the CEO and ask if this is the part we know how to do, or the part we are making up as we go. It is amazing how stunningly accurate this comment can be.

It happens every day in the executive suite, and it is something we should think about because it is one of the reasons that they let us in. They expect us to help them move the business ahead every single day, to help figure out what to do next.

Daily Intrusions

There are tasks CEOs face every day that only they can handle. These tasks are intrusions in the CEO's day. There are four kinds of daily task intrusions: soft intrusions, hard intrusions, nagging problems, and what we call, "career-defining moments."

Soft intrusions include:

- Negotiations with employees
- Anti-corporate government action
- Nagging negative news
- Personal, professional, or corporate embarrassment—real or potential
- Managing the moral decision-making elements of leadership
- Rumors
- Unfounded or even founded allegations

Hard intrusions are more operational:

- A major stock price drop
- Job actions and walkouts
- Major product market loss or product failures
- Other serious market problems
- Departure of a giant client or customer
- Failure to gain crucial government approvals
- Mergers or takeovers
- Preparing for litigation

Nagging problems are:

- Aggressive activist attacks, maybe on an individual executive or one board members
- Disgruntled employee or whistleblower problems
- Negative trends in stock and business performance
- Persistent bad news
- Bullying on social media. These kinds of problems just sort of hang on and gnaw at the CEO every day.

Career-defining moments:

- Sudden stock price manipulation
- Criminal indictments
- Serious people failures
- Serious high-profile product failures, recalls, or deaths
- Embarrassing, needless, obviously stupid events for which the CEO is held accountable.

It is amazing what takes up the CEO's day but they generally fall into these four categories. It is helpful to use this category approach, because among your key functions is to identify, prevent, preempt, correct, suggest, or develop solution options for these daily problems and issues.

Why Leaders Fail

While we are talking about the CEO's main responsibilities, we also ought to talk about why CEOs lose their positions. At the present time, CEO turnover is starting to rise again after a down period during the COVID-19 pandemic. *Forbes* and other business media occasionally publish studies of the principal reasons CEOs get fired or are asked to resign. Five reasons tend to stand out.

1. Failure to Deliver on What Was Promised or Expected When They Got the Job

Boards of directors of businesses and organizations, as well as shareholders, are becoming increasingly impatient with nonperformance. The risks are high, the stakes are high, mistakes are costly, and there is a lot of talent available these days to take on the visions of organizations. As a trusted advisor, one of your key roles is to look for signs of nonperformance and bring them to the attention of those you are counseling.

2. Over-Optimism

CEOs and those around them tend to be overly optimistic in the way they describe their progress, minimize obstacles, underrate opposition forces, and deny the weaknesses in their organization, structure, strategies, and operations. Eventually, the metrics of performance or the truth from the line managers of a business will reduce and clarify whatever over-optimism CEOs and their advisors might provide. Here again, the role of the Trusted Strategic Advisor is to take a pragmatic view of performance and accomplishment. This guidance helps the CEO gravitate more toward reality.

3. People Problems

The CEO's key job is to find and put the right people in the right jobs to accomplish the objectives. Failure to accomplish this will cause the organizational effort to fragment or simply not to form. Teamwork suffers; people stop trying to pull together. Important talent becomes demotivated and unproductive—or leaves the organization. New talent becomes nearly impossible to recruit.

4. Distractions

This usually means too many roles outside the company on boards and commissions, giving speeches, or other outside interests that get in the way of the CEO focusing on what needs to be done when big decisions have to be made. Jim often characterizes these behaviors as being AWOL, Absent Without Leave.

5. Stuck in the Mud

Usually a mysterious category, but it has an obvious result—nothing is happening, progress is not being made, and people may be leaving. For some reason, extremely talented individuals in one business environment failed by creating paralysis in another.

This list of reasons CEOs get fired shows clearly what is expected of them. They need to deliver on the bold promises they made or that the board expects in order to move the organization ahead, face and clearly define reality, build effective teams, stay focused, and get good at figuring out what to do next.

How Leaders Achieve Success

Today's leaders have to be successful. They will pay attention to you if you can demonstrate that you have a good sense of what matters to them in achieving success.

Every CEO and leader assembles their own set of ingredients to help drive them toward the success they seek. Some of these ingredients are intellectual, some of these ingredients are financial, some of these ingredients are emotional, and many of these ingredients are behavioral.

In observing leaders, and simply tying common behaviors to those who succeed, and the lack of certain behaviors to those who fail or who fail to succeed significantly, it appears to us that there are six crucial ingredients to CEO success. The absence of any one of these will severely threaten the sense of success to be achieved, and perhaps even trigger additional negative behaviors by boards of directors and stakeholders like employees, customers, or shareholders. These six ingredients are really powerful in terms of CEO success. And so they matter a great deal to leaders.

1. Focus

It is what Price Pritchett calls the 95/5 rule. Ninety-five percent of what we do every day probably does not really matter much. Focus means relentlessly dealing with the 5% that is really crucial, really essential, and really important. We believe this is one of the most powerful disciplines of leadership—and when you consider the daily intrusions outlined above, often very difficult to achieve.

2. Limit the Number of Objectives to Be Achieved

A leader can accomplish only a limited number of incremental steps every day. And, it makes little sense to commit to a whole series of major objectives recognizing that they will be unable to manage the many details necessary to get them all done. Fewer important objectives to achieve means a manageable number of incremental steps can be accomplished. Success is more likely.

3. Build Support and Create Followers

One of the great downfalls of CEOs is the inability to manage the people dimension. There have to be supportive people in place around these CEOs to make their work successful. People can stay together in support of the CEO if they can communicate constantly. Maintaining followers is a daily process because most employees do not know, cannot know, do not care, or cannot care about what the CEO cares about or does. It is up to the CEO to verbally communicate what matters with great intensity, continuity, and repetition. It is up to the Trusted Strategic Advisor to help design the key decisions, strategies, and messaging to keep the pack moving in the right direction.

4. Fix What Is Broken Fast

Do it now. When things go in the ditch, pull them out now. If it is even likely that something might be cracked, broken, or slipping into the ditch, CEOs act preemptively to fix it now. A related concept is to change fast. In other words, if things are moving in the marketplace in ways that have not been anticipated, leaders move appropriately, move quickly, and in some degree try to move ahead of the game once they understand the direction it is going, or figure out a better direction. Fix it now; challenge it now; start it now; stop it now. Leaders learn that most strategies fail because of timidity, hesitation, and indecision.

5. Finish What You Start

The number one reason that CEOs lose their jobs is because they do not or cannot get done what they promised when they got the job. So the skill here is to do less but get more of those fewer goals done. And for the key advisor in particular, this is a very tough challenge because most are idea people. We are the folks who are always thinking up new things to do. For the boss, this is a problem. You walk in bright-eyed and bushy-tailed for your Monday briefing session, and you spend half that time laying out new ideas for the boss to think about. The moment you leave the room, the boss almost explodes.

6. Start to Stop What's Not Working or Not Going to Succeed

Failure to make the tough decisions early can leave a leader with a list of wonderful achievements and a list of abject failures. Organizational attention almost always becomes captured by the failures, regardless of the levels of success achieved. Mistakes and unexpected outcomes tend to suck up resources from other more successful projects.

Be very careful here; many of the most important inventions and discoveries ever have come from mistakes and unexpected results. If you're interested in what some of them are just Google, Successful Mistakes in History or a similar title. Then you'll see what an amazing list of things we have that have saved our lives and done other things for us. All are the result of mistakes and errors, as opposed to planned scientific protocols.

Not only has the CEO failed to finish the work they were expected to complete last week, but now there are four or five new ideas on the desk, which, it would appear, others fully expect the CEO to work with and potentially accomplish. Before a CEO can get to next week, this week and last week have to be finished first.

Ask yourself what you do when you are at the table with the CEO or senior leaders. Do you push your staff function, or do you help them focus, keep objectives limited, build support, fix what is broken, and finish the work at hand? If you are not doing one of these six things, they probably think you are wasting their time.

The CEO's daily educational track is what they learned from their peers, and from the one, two, or three people who are guiding touchstones in their lives. Do you know who your CEO's touchstone people are? Do you know who the people are that the CEO turns to when there is a crucial question to ask or when they want to avoid internal resources? Can you help reverse the inevitable isolation from useful daily information the CEO often feels?

Jim is occasionally asked, "Does the trusted advisor need to be smarter than the leader him/herself?" The answer is that the vast majority of Trusted Strategic Advisors have little, if any, desire to be a leader in the first place. Their sole goal is to be the best number two, the best associate/assistant, the best helper, encourager, and success driver possible. Well, you might ask, "Why would one want to become a trusted advisor instead of the leader, in their own right?" The answer seems to be that leadership is simply beyond that which trusted advisors seek to achieve. In reality, for those advisors who wish to be leaders, there is ample opportunity to move in that direction, and those CEOs and leaders they have helped will undoubtedly be instrumental in moving these people along.

In our experience, it is far less likely that a consultant will become a leader over time, simply due to the fascinating power, access, and insight being close to leaders tends to generate. In reality there are far greater opportunities for trusted advisors than there are leadership positions available. Adjusting one's expectations and temperament to these very influential positions provides a very interesting, dynamic, meaningful, and important professional life.

Implications and Applications for the Advisor

At the outset of this chapter, we suggested that you focus on the realities that surround the leaders at the top of the organizational pyramid. Of course, they enjoy great power and prestige. But that aura of power is tempered by the advisor's perspective and temperament. Top leaders are under increasing pressure, and their job security is often tenuous. They may have some vision of where they want to go, but they know they need help to see the future. They will be making up a significant portion of the goals as they go along. They can feel tremendously isolated, and the levers at their command can only nudge the organization to change direction.

If you are serious about advising people at senior levels, one of your great preoccupations must become the study of leaders, leadership, and leadership activity. It is surprising how few staff people truly study their leaders and leadership, what operating people do every day, and how leaders become and stay leaders. Studying leadership involves a very practical and ongoing curiosity about:

- Who leaders are
- Where they come from
- What their relationships are
- How they came to be where they are

It also requires understanding what leaders are trying to accomplish, what motivates them, how they think about various issues, topics, and circumstances, and the behaviors you can expect to forecast as you get to know them.

Question for You to Consider

How do you study leadership? Our suggestion is to begin by looking at the kind of literature and sources leaders have and use to be informed. Here is a list of publications CEOs tell us they routinely review:

- *Baron's Magazine*
- *Berkshire Hathaway's Annual Report* (any year)

- *BoardRoom Magazine*
- *Directors and Boards Magazine*
- *Executive Book Summaries* (monthly summaries of new business books)
- *Fast Company Magazine*
- *Forbes Magazine*
- *Fortune Magazine*
- *Harvard Business Review*
- *Sloan Management Review*
- *The Wall Street Journal* (every day)
- Writings and books by former CEOs and other leaders

When queried about the most important business writers and thinkers, those they pay attention to, these are the names that crop up continuously:

- Peter F. Drucker
- Indra Nooyi (influential voice on corporate governance)
- Mary Barra (first female CEO of a major auto company—General Motors)
- Kara Swisher (leading interrogator of Silicon Valley power)
- John Kotter (Harvard)
- Warren Bennis (consultant)
- James Collins (consultant)
- Sheryl Sandberg (architect of Meta's business model)
- Stephen Covey
- Tom Peters (business philosopher)
- Joseph Rotman (Rotman School of Management, University of Toronto)
- Noel Tichy (author, lecturer, human resource executive)

Some of Fred's favorites include:

- Retired U.S. Army Four-Star General Stanley McChrystal
- Retired U.S. Navy Four-Star Admiral James Stavridis

Among the few historical individuals whose biographies leaders are often interested in are:

- Winston Churchill
- Benjamin Franklin
- Alexander Hamilton
- General Douglas MacArthur
- Theodore Roosevelt

Pick your list. All of these kinds of writings are extremely helpful in understanding the mentality, attitudes, behaviors, and aspirations of leaders.

Studying leadership should lead you to discover more interesting ways to be of service, create more powerful and purposeful ideas and suggestions, and a deeper understanding of how those you advise, and you can do bigger and better things on a regular basis. Only then can you become a trusted advisor. In the next chapter, we will look at what leaders will expect from you in this role.

2 What Leaders Expect

Chapter Outline

Seven key expectations executives have for advisors, five types of effective advice, and the talents and abilities expected of advisors.

Now that you have a better sense of the CEO's world, it is time to think about what the boss will expect of you.

One of Fred's axioms, about which he has published, taught, and preached extensively, is that you can't move people unless you meet them where they are. This is especially true when influencing leaders.

As always, we begin by looking at those expectations from the boss's special perspective—their goals, desires, attitudes, aptitudes, and attributes, including the 25% of the big decisions that CEOs and other leaders will be making up as they go. For the trusted advisor, this is a permanent mindset. A theme that runs throughout every chapter in this book and throughout the work of the Trusted Strategic Advisor is the concept of having a management mindset. This mindset is a combination of factors, some of which you have already been introduced to: the concept of reading significant leadership publications, studying leadership and leaders, and developing some real expertise in the business activities, strategies, and processes of the organizations whose leaders you are advising.

Of all the shortcomings operating people complain about, it is that staff people fail to gain any depth of knowledge in the actual work of the business whose leaders they staff. Virtually every truly successful trusted advisor we have observed or worked with has mentioned their desire to learn and apply key operational information, strategy, and background. Doing this is among the most powerful relationship builders they and you have experienced.

An up-and-coming advisor friend of Jim's called one day and told him she was being considered for an operating position. She was curious about his thinking about leaving a staff role and going into operations. His immediate response was, "Do it. Do it today, if you can, before it goes to somebody else." Aside from getting advanced degrees in law or business or some other field, taking an operating position where you are meeting a payroll and running a business or business unit is one of the most extraordinarily powerful experience a staff person can accomplish. "Wait a minute," she said. "They're asking me to manage a division of garbage truck drivers." Jim's response was, "So? Isn't this where the money comes from? Every time they throw a bucket of trash in the back, it is cash in the register, yes? This may well be among the most important roles in the company."

She said, "I hadn't quite thought of it that way. But there are two problems. First, I'm a relatively young woman about to manage 300 men who are garbage men. The second problem, I have no operational experience, only public affairs experience in this industry. Will these guys ever pay attention to me?" Jim suggested to her that she find a way to get some experience by the time she accepts the position and the time she actually has to go to work, which was approximately 45 days.

Jim had pretty much forgotten about it when the phone rang a few months later, and there she was reporting on her first 30 days running the Collections Division.

Jim asked, "How's it going?" She said, "I think I got off on the right foot. After I talked to you, I talked to my boss, and he enrolled me in garbage truck driving school; I got my Cartage License. I put it to use my first day of work. The day before I was to arrive for my first day at the new job, which was a location remote from corporate headquarters, I signed out a garbage truck. And, as I pulled into my new office parking lot, it seemed as though everybody was in the lot waiting for me to arrive. I hit the horn, made a quick U-turn, and backed my garbage truck perfectly into my parking spot. There was a great cheer. So far things are going really well."

Learn something that matters about the business, and you will go a very long way toward gaining the respect and connection you will need to become a Trusted Strategic Advisor, or a confident and helpful operator.

The Boss's Special Perspective

It is the CEO who has the most open and complete view of the organization. Consider the CEO to be at the top of the pyramid of your organization, sitting on what is today a very sharp point, as a matter of fact. In this uncomfortable position, they do have a clearer view than anyone else of every aspect of the business's operations. Everyone else who is hanging onto the sides of the pyramid has at least a partially obstructed view of the business. Moreover, every staff person who supports a senior executive has a view that is biased by their staff function.

David A. Nadler, writing in *Harvard Business Review*, illustrated the inherent uniqueness of the top position by identifying five "no one else" factors that dominate the CEO's circumstances.[1] No one else, says Nadler:

- Has a greater need for sources of unbiased information.
- Needs to hear hard truths faster.
- Is such a lightning rod for criticism.
- Is the final arbiter in so many vital business decisions.
- Is the subject of so many statements beginning with "no one else."

On the other hand, "everyone else" on the side of this pyramid is busy holding on to preserve their position in the organization or looking for ways to move higher.

In the past, it was the duty of those on the pyramid, just under the CEO, to help stabilize this individual during tough times, crosswinds, gusty weather, and white water for the benefit of the entire organization. In many respects, the point on which the CEO sits today has gotten even sharper: those directly below the CEO are far less inclined to be stabilizers, particularly if something is happening that may diminish their chances of succeeding to the top of the pyramid. They are busy organizing for their own possible succession, protecting their turf, and, perhaps, keeping a peer from gaining any additional advantage.

The clear view of the CEO turns out to be an enormous advantage, whatever this individual decides to do and however they decide to get their work done. This pyramid has sometimes been called a "monkey tree." That is, if you are on the top of this tree looking down, what you see looking up at you is a bunch of smiling monkey faces. But, if you are on the monkey tree somewhere down below, looking up, your view is quite different. Clearly, the best place on the tree to be is at the very top.

The Counselor's Prime Directive

Having been advisors virtually our entire careers, we have to confess our ongoing admiration for those at the top of the pyramid. Real leaders listen, hear, seek out many voices, and then, from that huge menu of ideas and concepts, they extract key insights or inspirations that will move an organization into the future. This is a crucial and amazing capacity of leadership. Few consultants and advisors have either this skill or temperament.

After watching thousands of consultants and advisors at work, it strikes us that very few actually have the capacity to lead because very few are willing to readily accept the ideas of others or include them in what they are trying to accomplish. This acceptance and willingness to seek advice and inclusion is one genius of leadership. It is about the leader's ability to sift, to sort, to distill, to stratify, and to prioritize the ingredients of the future and then combine certain ingredients to fuel progress.

The trusted advisor has to be aware that whining, negativity, and competition for the boss's attention often block the advisor's ability to influence key strategic decisions. These staff behaviors are among the most irritating, relationship-corroding events between advisors and leaders.

Another relationship-corroding phenomenon is resistance to the presence of an outside advisor. For example, when Fred arrives to advise senior leaders, staff often feel threatened and fear that he is there to displace them and their relationship with their bosses. But pretty quickly they learn that they can truly value his presence. Sometimes Fred even says to them in private, "I want to help you do your job, and help you build your relationship with your boss. My role is to help the boss, and those who advise the boss, including you, to be more successful." Many are initially skeptical. But when they see Fred living true to this promise, they tend to embrace his presence.

Seeing things from the boss's perspective means welcoming advice, even if that advice comes from someone else or a competing interest. You understand why the boss needs to have it.

There are five useful types of effective advice:

1. Practical advice means just that—tasks that are achievable, positive in nature, and that employees and even critics can endorse to some degree. Pragmatic advice recognizes that only certain outcomes are possible, that no matter how spiffy, creative, or exciting your ideas might be, those affected by the advice as well as those acting on the advice will look at it from the perspective of whether it can actually work in their real world.
2. Purposeful advice has self-evident forward focus and positive momentum. Counselors and consultants are strategic operational assets. When activated, strategic assets are fundamentally positive and energize the organization and its constituencies.
3. Focused advice means just that, advice that is understandable, shows the way, helps the client or customer think and act in the future tense, and works toward a few (or one) important goals everyone recognizes.
4. Fair advice means that which is politically acceptable (as opposed to factually correct) and politically useful (as opposed to manipulative or politically disruptive).
5. Ethical advice, which includes:
   a. Finding the truth as soon as possible.
   b. Raising tough questions promptly.

c. Teaching by emphasizing wrong way/right way options for vocalized core business values and ideals constantly.
d. Walking the talk; being accessible.
e. Helping, expecting, and enforcing ethical leadership.
f. Preserving, protecting, defending, and fostering ethical pathways to the top of the organization.
g. Being a cheerleader, model, and teacher of ethical behavior.
h. Making values at least equal to profits or personal gain.
i. Valuing everyone and being respectful.

There are lots of distractions in consulting, and many clients have great difficulties, problems, shortcomings, and blind spots. The consultant's obligation is to identify and provide candid, constructive advice that fills those deficiencies, strengthens the shortcomings, and reduces blind spots while stabilizing or moving the organization toward tomorrow.

How the Boss Measures Advice

Those strategic few who spend a fair amount of time talking with, working with, and counseling CEOs, senior leaders, and other operating executives, quickly learn the strategic expectations of bosses. They understand that the leader values only advice that has a positive impact on the organization.

> Before offering ideas, concepts, and recommendations to the senior leaders, ask yourself these five questions:
>
> - Does it help the boss achieve their objectives and goals?
> - Does it help the organization achieve its goals?
> - If the answers to numbers one and two are "yes," is the project truly needed?
> - What aspect of the business will fail or fail to progress if your recommendation is ignored or delayed?
> - How does this suggestion save money, make money, or conserve money?

If you can keep your focus on these critical questions, your advice will be relevant. This approach puts you squarely in the CEO's shoes, looking at his/her tasks, challenges, and loneliness from a management perspective.

The Counselor's Commitment

The chances are you will be sought after, respected, and have important influence on what the CEO does, what the organization does, and the success the organization achieves if you live by the principles ofThe Counselor's Commitment.

> Those who successfully serve others have a work attitude that says:
>
> 1. When I am here, working for you is number one.
> 2. I plan to be here a lot and, if necessary, available the rest of the time as well.
> 3. I am committed to extensive independent reading, discussion, issue sensitivity, and personal learning that is of value to those I coach and counsel.
> 4. I will take the initiative to help those I coach and counsel move in useful new directions and rely far more on foresight than hindsight.
> 5. I recognize that going even a small extra distance will be the difference between mundane and magnificent results. Extra effort, extra sensitivity, and extra focus is what makes the difference from the client's perspective.

What Bosses Expect from Strategic Advisors

What is really expected of you as an advisor? What are the obligations of those who advise CEOs, based on what they expect?

Here are seven important behavior expectations CEOs look for in the Trusted Strategic Advisor:

1. Real-Time Advice
2. Candor
3. Coaching at Every Encounter
4. Consequence Analysis, Being Insightful
5. Knowing What Is Important
6. Early Warning
7. Knowing What to Do Next

Real-Time Advice

You have to be able to give advice on the spot. If your methodology is to walk in, ask questions, take some notes, leave, think about things for a while, and come back, you are going to find that they have moved on by the time you return. That is because at the CEO level, decisions are made and actions are taken pretty much in real time. You have to be able to give advice on the spot or you will only be invited back when the boss has an assignment. You will only be invited back when the boss has figured out what they want you to do.

Candor

Jim defines candor as "truth with an attitude, delivered right now!" It is being super honest, promptly, and supporting that honesty with collateral information that matters. A candid advisor is willing to talk about anything, at any time, under any circumstances—and is willing to build transparency into every process, question, issue, or problem. But it is important to avoid conflating "truth with attitude" and "truth with arrogance." The attitude is always positive and obviously in the service of the leader's best interest.

Coaching at Every Encounter

Take the opportunity to guide, to counsel, to redirect or direct the CEO in ways that are beneficial from their perspective, every time you are together. Suggest things that matter. Leaders expect it.

If you are in the room with the CEO or leaders, you are expected to speak unless your role is designated as that of an observer. Your non-speaking role will need to be explained by someone, preferably you or the boss or client. You are in the presence of leadership to provide something useful or be gone.

CEOs and leaders do notice whether or not you say something that matters even when you are in situations with large numbers of consultants and voices present. They have a special sense about who is there and who is speaking. Even though some of these meetings can be intimidating—if not because of the CEO, directly, then because of the level, skill, and intensity of others in the room—if you are there, you are expected to offer useful advice on the spot. Failure to do so may mean losing your place at subsequent meetings until you can re-earn an invitation, if that is even possible.

Consequence Analysis, Being Insightful

You have to be able to interpret for CEOs what different aspects of a situation mean, and the likely consequences and impacts of various choices. What is going on in the company's environment? Being a consequence analyst is taking information that exists but may seem unrelated or even commonplace and extracting more value in the context of running the business. You need to be a decision-clarifier, a translator. You are helping the boss understand what is moving in their direction, what needs to be decided, and even the priority of the decisions that need to be made. Outside their presence, you become an interpreter and explainer of the boss's actions and decisions for other publics and constituencies.

For much of his career Fred has described this role as being a kind of applied anthropologist. Like an anthropologist, the strategic advisor does field work to understand the dynamics of groups that matter to the CEO: their values, their fears, their desires, how they make decisions, and how their behavior is triggered. The applied part involves advising on a range of options, and the consequences—both intended and unintended—of each. If we do X, this is what we can expect . . . If we do Y, this is what we can expect . . . If we do Z, this is what we can expect . . . This ability to project—to predict—the future, to be a consequence analyst, is a core differentiator of the strategic advisor. And when leaders see that advisors have this ability, they often seek out the advisors to be thought partners in the moment.

One of Fred's clients, a senior officer in the US military, called Fred out of the blue one day. He said, "I've been struggling over an important decision I need to make. I wonder if we can rub our brains together." It's an indelicate way of saying it, but the client realized that he needed someone to think with him; to guide him in his decision-making process. After about an hour of reviewing options and consequences, the officer said, "Great. I've got this. I know what I need to do."

Knowing What Is Important

The filtration of information becomes so severe as it nears the top of an organization that most senior executives, but especially the CEO, feel, with concern, that what they receive is boiled down, oversimplified, sanitized, and detoxified. One of the Trusted Strategic Advisor's crucial roles is making certain that key information makes it to the top very promptly, perhaps even ahead of everyone else in the organization.

Early Warning

Since the trusted advisor has a different perspective of the interests of those they advise, it is likely that they will be in early possession of information that could be helpful in avoiding danger or serious threats. This attention may also provide early recognition that certain projects, programs, or ideas are failing and need to be stopped before they waste any more resources or send any more negative signals.

Knowing What to Do Next

A significant number of the decisions CEOs make are based on their ability to see where the organization is headed, understanding the real-time assets and liabilities of the organization, and how to combine those assets and abilities with potential opportunities. Still, the uncertainty of leadership always benefits from useful, sensible suggestions about what the next steps or increments might be. This is among the greatest contributions Trusted Strategic Advisors can make.

Talents Advisors Need

Successfully meeting the expectations of CEOs and leaders requires six special abilities: initiative, inspiration, intuition, loyalty, urgency, and, maybe surprisingly, inconsistency.

Initiative

The most common criticism we hear about outside and inside advisors is that although ideas abound, few advisors seem capable of picking up an idea, developing it, and moving it forward without prompting or specific direction.

Initiative at very senior levels carries significant risks and, quite often, the higher the altitude the more risk-adverse individuals become. Since leaders, for the most part, spend time waiting for things to happen, finish, or progress, those advisors with initiative earn higher levels of respect, attention, and often better pay.

Inspiration

Inspiration is the ability to positively energize others in ways that benefit them emotionally and privately from their perspective. Those who inspire help others see (from their own perspectives) new truths and special insights that affect their emotions, behaviors, and beliefs. Identify those who inspire you.

Quite often, unless someone makes a comment or reveals themselves, inspiration is a private moment of revelation between the individual who presents the opportunity and the individuals who benefit. The isolation of leadership both triggers and inhibits the inspiration of new ideas and creative thinking. The Trusted Strategic Advisor brings the inspirational ingredient to each encounter they have with the boss and others.

This is a quality that can be learned and developed. The best way to learn to inspire is to observe those who inspire you. Learn how they do it. Focus on how they do it. Then do what they do and see if it works for you. Then use that knowledge to develop your own inspirational style. Inspire others. It is truly a gift that is appreciated although often not acknowledged.

Early in his career Fred was inspired by Jim. Fred spent much of his time studying how Jim inspired others, then trying to do the same thing, but in his own voice. Over time, Fred expanded his universe of inspiring behaviors building on those he learned from Jim, doing the same, and also learning by studying other mentors and colleagues.

Intuition

Intuition is among the most unique of the advisor's special abilities. It is difficult to develop and to cultivate. This exceptional quality of the trusted advisor—the ability to "see" solutions and next-step elements with little evidence and data—is a highly prized skill. You can discipline yourself to develop your intuitive abilities.

On the other hand, those who run organizations, especially large organizations, have a limited tolerance for intuitive solutions and recommendations. Managers today pride themselves on fact-based decision-making.

But it's one thing to develop an insight based on intuition; it's another to be able to explain that insight in a way that leaders respond to. Let the intuition be the starting point but explain the insight without using the vocabulary of intuition. Present intuitive recommendations using a process approach so that you can be understood and your ideas acted upon by those you counsel. This includes being able to forecast consequences. See the Three-Minute Drill in Chapter 9.

Loyalty

The loyalty of the Trusted Strategic Advisor is based on three factors:

- **a.** Alignment of fundamental principles of behavior, goals, and aspirations.
- **b.** The productive and constructive chemistry created between individuals who work well together toward mutually agreed-upon goals.
- **c.** A relationship based on candor and responsiveness to issues and questions that matter. Loyalty is the conscientious alignment of goals, interests, and actions.

Loyalty is an intentional element in a relationship. It is a key ingredient between the trusted advisor and those who are coached and counseled.

Advising at senior levels also automatically makes you the eyes and ears for those you counsel. It is a part of the information base that informs your advice. Successfully advising and coaching senior people requires a high level of personal candor, about the leaders themselves, and about the what and the why of what is happening around them. Loyalty is more than following, it is actively engaging in the successful progress of leadership ideas combined with continued verbalization and analysis of organizational behaviors, decisions, and actions.

The Loyalty Exception The loyalty exception refers to the fact that sometimes we stay and help people who either don't deserve it or who are having problems we think we can help with, but it never really works out that way. So the loyalty exception says if it is immoral, impossible, irregular, or unethical, you need to leave, rather than continue helping people in those positions.

Urgency

Time is the universal perishable. Urgency is achieved when time is, or is used as, a driving force. Urgency is created when the loss of time has real consequences. If things are important, it is because time is a big factor. If matters are urgent, it is because time may be running out. From an advisor's point of view, urgency means using time wisely by saying things powerfully and briefly. And by using the pressure of time to constructively increase the importance of all actions.

Setting priorities establishes a sense of urgency. Resolving issues and problems quickly and effectively also creates urgency. Applying pressure to get things done at the earliest possible time, often for the most important of reasons, creates urgency.

Urgency is a double-edged tool. Used to motivate, inspire, and energize, urgency can be a constructive and productive force. Used to intimidate, badger, and bully, urgency can be destructive, corrosive, and have long-term negative impact.

Inconsistency

One of the greatest gifts of the strategist is the ability, in fact, the intention to see things from multiple points of view. Sometimes, this may seem to be recommending things that are inconsistent. Organizations that seek consistency rarely are successful for lengthy periods of time. The hallmarks of inconsistency are:

- Always seeking alternatives.
- Believing in laggership and entropy, as opposed to speed and stealth.
- Intentionally explore different views and analysis.
- Questions all assumptions.
- Simplify, simplify, simplify.

Do You Fit in the CEO Environment?

Now let us talk about you and whether or not you fit in this environment. Here are some serious questions:

1. Do you study leadership and the process of leadership?
2. Do you care about these senior people?
3. Do you have or can you develop a real interest and some expertise in the fields of interest of those you intend to advise?
4. Do you care about what the CEO needs to have or get done?
5. Can you set your problems and issues aside long enough to deal with their problems, goals, and questions?
6. Can you manage your own ego involvement in an environment where there are even bigger egos than yours?
7. Can you make the Counselor's Commitment?

In the next chapter, we will take a look at the trusted advisor's critical tasks. You rarely find them listed in any job description or anywhere in your organization. Sometimes the boss will clearly spell out what they want; but most often it will be unspoken. It does not matter; you will need to figure it out.

Resources

Here are several resources we have found useful for learning about consulting and coaching CEOs and leaders:

- *Flawless Consulting: A Guide to Getting Your Expertise Used*, Fourth Edition, Peter Block, Wiley, 2023.
- *The Flawless Consulting Fieldbook and Companion: A Guide to Understanding Your Expertise*, Second Edition, Peter Block, assisted by Andrea Markowitz, Jossey-Bass Pfeiffer, 2001.
- *Coaching for Leadership: How the World's Greatest Coaches Help Leaders Learn*, edited by Marshall Goldsmith, Laurence Lyons, and Alyssa Freas, Jossey-Bass Pfeiffer, 2000.
- *Control Your Destiny or Someone Else Will: How Jack Welch Created $400 Billion of Value by Transforming GE*, Noel M. Tichy and Stratford Sherman, Lulu Publishing, 2018.
- *Leaders Eat Last: Why Some Teams Pull Together and Others Don't,* Simon Sinek, Portfolio, 2017.
- *Lean In: Women, Work, and the Will to Lead*, Sheryl Sandberg, Knopf, 2013.
- *The 21 Irrefutable Laws of Leadership* by John C. Maxwell, Thomas Nelson, 2007.
- *Dare to Lead Brave Work. Tough Conversations. Whole Hearts*, Brené Brown, Random House, 2018.
- *Primal Leadership: Unleashing the Power of Emotional Intelligence,* Daniel Goleman, Harvard Business Review Press, 2016.

3 Achieving Maximum Impact

Chapter Outline

How to gain senior manager confidence, speaking management's language, annoying staff habits to avoid, and the five areas bosses need feedback on every day.

Viewing the world from a leadership rather than a staff perspective is the crucial prerequisite for establishing a sound relationship. There is always that nagging thought at the back of the boss's mind about consultants, counselors, and staff people: "Do these people really know what I do here every day, as they offer advice and counsel? Do they even care about what I want to accomplish?" We explained how to answer these questions in the previous two chapters. In this chapter, the focus shifts to your behavior and how you can achieve maximum impact as a trusted advisor.

Being listened to and having impact requires that you gain the confidence of top leadership, understand and speak their language, avoid the typical staff shortcomings that annoy bosses, respect the boss's time, develop the discipline to structure your presentations, give useful feedback, and meet other expectations.

Gaining and Keeping the Confidence of Senior People

Typically, our arrival at a client location triggers a variety of individuals being tasked with briefing us on the situation: the individuals involved, the various relationships of the players, and whatever other information these high-level staffers think is important for us, as outsiders, to know. Frequently, the focus of these discussions shifts from the problem at hand to criticism of leaders in terms of assigning blame for the current situation, speculation about causes and sources for the existing environment, miscellaneous indictments of style, failure to adapt or adopt preventative or preemptive measures, plus a credible staff-level assessment of leadership.

These are typical staff habits. And while we do listen to these discussions and, to some degree, take these matters into account, our inner voice would love to say, "If I were your boss hearing this discussion, I would fire you on the spot." That is because your boss needs you to fill in the blind spots, shore up the weaknesses, and find ways to overcome their deficiencies. It is one thing to notice the needs, deficiencies, and other problematic elements leaders suffer, but it is totally another to develop methods, options, techniques, and opportunities that address them constructively and promptly.

If you want to be listened to and have an impact, start where the boss believes they are. Focus, first and foremost, on establishing the relationship of trust and common direction with the boss. These are the relationship elements that matter. It is the mutual recognition of common direction that provides the platform for fixing various other shortcomings that may indeed be present. It may also illustrate that the concerns of other staff people are far less relevant to achieving the boss's goals.

Some years ago Jim was retained by a large corporation to coach the chairman in preparation for a lengthy television series on his life as a senior executive. The chairman was so busy that Jim scheduled three-hour sessions in a television studio to rehearse some of his stories and generally get him comfortable with what was going to happen. The first session was to be held in the headquarters building in Stamford, Connecticut. The chairman didn't show.

Nine days later, he had time on his schedule in San Francisco for a three-hour session. Jim traveled to San Francisco and got everything ready. The chairman didn't show.

A week later, a third session was scheduled in Dallas, Texas. Same routine, same drill. The chairman didn't show.

With just a handful of days to go before the actual taping was to begin, a session was scheduled in Stamford as a final attempt on the part of his staff to have him spend some time getting ready.

This was all the more interesting to Jim because he and the chairman actually had talked to each other and knew each other from earlier in their careers. But the chairman's schedule prevailed.

With 20 minutes left in a three-hour time period, the chairman came in the door, walked over to Jim, grabbed his hand, and said in his Texas drawl, "Hello, Jeem, I bet you thought I was ducking these sessions on purpose."

Jim's response was, "Well, Rocky, the thought crossed my mind." He went on to tell Jim that the problem with what his staff proposed for him, "media training," as he called it, was that when he spoke with his wife, her response was, "I've been married to you for 47 years and haven't been able to train you to do anything. How can someone you hardly know train you to be something different in just three hours?"

Rocky went on to tell Jim that he had learned in his life to pay attention to his wife, but he wanted to make certain that Jim did not take it personally that he had missed all the sessions.

Jim's response to Rocky was, "What I had in mind was more along the lines of coaching, just to get you more comfortable and ready to deal with the two days of videotaping that will occur at Public Broadcasting Studios." He replied, "Coaching! Well, I can always use some coaching." And so Jim and Rocky worked for the remaining time.

Following the airing of the program, Rocky's advisors sent him the videotapes to assess how the chairman had done. From the first moment he was on camera, you understood vividly why Wall Street, the company's shareholders, employees, and others so implicitly trusted him. In his rather folksy Texas manner, he spoke the truth at every turn. He said things that were important, and he clearly had a sense of where the company was heading.

Rather than write the extensive critique the client requested, Jim told the client staff they should use the tapes of his performances for training other executives about how to be an honest, honorable, extremely forthright and trustworthy visionary. Rocky was all of these.

It seemed that most of his advisors were from the East Coast, mainly New York and Connecticut. For some reason they felt that a "good ol' boy" from Texas, even though he was an extraordinarily successful businessperson, had to sound like he came from Connecticut to be an effective representative of the company. But Rocky knew what mattered, and he delivered.

For more than two decades Fred advised leaders of a large insurance company headquartered in the Midwest. For much of that time the company was Fred's largest client, and he spent lots of time on site. He worked with two successive CEOs and dozens of their senior leaders.

At one point he was asked to work with a newly promoted executive who had just assumed meaningful responsibilities. But the executive was resistant. The CEO told him to work with Fred anyway. Over time Fred detected the resistance fading. Then one day, surprisingly, the executive invited Fred and one of his colleagues to his house for dinner and to meet his wife. This was unusual.

They had a lovely dinner and conversation with the client and his wife. As he was walking them to the door afterward, the executive stopped and said he needed to confess something to them: "I've always been deeply skeptical of New York consultants—the Wise Men from the East—who come here and tell us what to do. But I've figured out why my company keeps you around."

Fred was eager to hear the rest. He asked, "And why is that?" His client replied, "You guys are really smart. But you don't make us feel as if we're dumb. When you're with us, you make us feel that we're really smart too."

Speak Management's Language

Some years ago during a presentation by a communications firm that had recently been acquired by one of the large international consulting companies, there was a fascinating discussion about how the communicators group was required to rethink their entire business model. They had two powerful objectives. The first was to describe their communications services, advice, and skills in much more management-oriented language. The second was to significantly reduce the number of potential service and counseling offerings so that all the consultants on the operating side of the firm and their client base could understand and utilize what was being offered, in a management context.

The exercise the acquired communications group went through was quite enlightening and its result was a focused list of services, expressed in management language and structured in ways that fit strategically into the other parts of the consulting operation. Here is how this new division described their management communication consulting practice areas:

- Strategic Planning *(formerly brainstorming and ideation)*
- Customer-Centered Re-engineering *(formerly customer service)*
- Executive and Management Development *(formerly training)*
- Staff Development *(formerly professional development)*
- Team Building *(new concept)*
- Organizational Operational Review and Analysis *(formerly communication audit)*
- Corporate Marketing and Communications *(same)*
- Crisis Consulting *(formerly crisis management)*
- Readiness Management and Issue Surveillance *(formerly issues management)*
- Employee Loyalty Building *(formerly internal communications)*

This example is a useful demonstration for other staff functions as well, whether you work in the legal arena, human resources, security, finance, or marketing, this sort of approach resonates with management and enforces a new level of discipline on the staff function to look at things more specifically from the management perspective. The benefit is the reduction of those elements that are either too driven by professional jargon from a staff perspective or just simply less relevant. Take the time to look at the services you offer and recast them effectively in recognizable management language. If you find them difficult to translate into management language, what you are developing may be too staff-oriented. Let it go, or fix it.

Work Against the Patterns That Bother Bosses

In talking with chief executives and leaders, specifically about advice they get both internally and externally, a pattern of frustrations surfaces relatively quickly. These are the most frequently mentioned frustrations. You would be well advised to avoid them.

1. **Unintelligible, therefore unusable, approaches.**

   If you want something done by an operating person, you need to describe it appropriately. Consider the earlier example with Rocky. He was among the most accomplished executives in his industry, who was also in his seventies, and whose performance clearly indicated his accomplishment. The use of the term "training," the idea of being "trained" for something, was simply unintelligible. As Rocky admitted, successful executives bristle at the idea of being trained, but welcome and often seek out the opportunity to be coached.
2. **More ideas and concepts than can possibly be achieved or even considered.**

   Remember the most important reasons CEOs lose their jobs relate to failure to perform. If your methodology is to suggest new ways of doing things, or simply new things to do, you would be well advised to emphasize what needs to get done smarter, in a more focused way, and that is doable. And what has yet to be completed rather than putting even one or two new ideas on the boss's desk.
3. **Time wasting and non-specific (purposeless) conversations.**

   Even if it is the boss who brings up vacations, the family, what seems like chit chat, the trusted advisor's role is to keep these encounters focused on what truly matters when getting things done. Yes, it is true, over time, you will develop a relationship where a lot of personal information is known and seems appropriate to discuss, but our advice remains, keep these meetings and encounters as focused and professional as possible. Keep your actual role in focus at all times.
4. **Information that is late, incomplete, and with some key facts and data or interpretations apparently being purposely withheld.**

   Senior executives already know that the information they get is filtered, detoxified, and often pretty harmless. One of your most important currencies is candor: this important, concise, prompt disclosure of things you know that the boss should know. Information withheld or that is late for whatever reason reflects on the trust in your relationship. Even just a couple of incidents where the feeling persists on the part of the boss that you are intentionally failing to be forthcoming, and your invitations will decline.

5. **Information that is already known or could be thought up independently.**

   Stick to what matters. If it is something you know they know, move on. Count on it; you are wasting their time. Avoid doing that or risk losing a good part of your relationship.

6. **Giving only partial input, apparently on the assumption that the boss knows more than they do, or should know more than they do.**

   In Chapter 9, we talk about a structure for giving advice with options. This was designed to prevent providing only partial information. To avoid leaving out key information, talk in terms of timelines or priorities. What should be done first, second, or third, or apply a calendar or a clock to the information you have to share. This way, things the boss already knows get put in a new, useful, more strategic context.

7. **Reluctance to be candid.**

   This behavior is a relationship killer . . . Whether it is fear, lack of preparation, or simply timidity, lack of candor is the fastest way to become disemployed as a Trusted Strategic Advisor. If you want to be there, be ready, be actively engaged, and tell the truth promptly.

The problem with these behaviors and approaches is that they distract and irritate top executives and erect barriers to taking your advice or even taking you seriously.

Talk and Write to Time

Avoid the face-time fantasy. Too often, staff people estimate their value based on the number of minutes or hours they spend in the presence of, or interacting with, senior people. The only face time that really matters, truly, is when the staff person is giving useful advice to an organizational leader. It is true that these leaders often ask personal and personable questions. They appear to have a genuine interest in the individual who is advising them, and they really may. It certainly does happen and it is certainly possible, but generally, for the senior-most executives, it is far less about getting personal than about gaining key information to stay in or get ahead of the game.

Always talk to time rather than filling time with talk. Find ways to limit what you talk about so that whatever your discussion covers, you are ready to provide information in a format and fashion that is direct, helpful, instructive, and trustable.

Talking to time means remembering that, in English-speaking cultures, we speak about 150 words per minute. Most also read at the same speed. Every document, every script, every written piece of information should be screened for its time requirement. This can be done very easily by putting a word count (using your word count computer function) at the top of each page or document. Divide that word count number by 150, and you have the number of minutes it will take someone to read the document either to themselves or out loud to someone else.

The more important the decision or bigger the question or issue, the more likely it is that action will be pushed off until it has to be dealt with on an urgent or even panicky basis. The challenge, then, is to structure advice in a potent verbal or written format that saves time. The Three-Minute Drill, discussed in Chapter 9, if you can commit to using it, will change your relationship with your boss dramatically and help you have a much higher level of personal self-confidence. It will help everyone you advise.

Give Useful Feedback

To stay on course, and to continue the evolution of their leadership, CEOs and managers need clear, useful, relevant feedback every day. Few CEOs can easily obtain information meeting this criterion on their own. Bosses need:

1. Data feedback
2. Perception analysis

3. Gossip
4. Some perspective on what needs to happen next
5. People assessments, every day

As we have pointed out, one of the more surprising realities of being the CEO or top executive is that at this level, the kinds of information they need changes. Rather than lots of detail and specific information, CEOs and senior leaders need more evaluative and strategically relevant information. One thing we know at this altitude is that the information that CEOs and top managers get has been sanitized, organized, homogenized, and often made as inoffensive and generalized as possible. The feedback role of the Trusted Strategic Advisor is one of the most crucial ingredients of an ongoing productive relationship with top management. You are the eyes and ears of organizational leadership. You are also the mouthpiece sometimes. Often, while you are observing and collecting information and data, you find yourself, in return, interpreting, explaining, elaborating, or forecasting issues and actions of top executive decision-making. This goes with the territory.

Whenever we hear an advisor tell us that she feels like a snitch, or that his assignment should not include observing and reporting back to the boss on what fellow employees are saying, doing, or feeling, we know this person will fail as a strategic advisor because they are failing the boss. The Trusted Strategic Advisor has an affirmative obligation to pay attention to the surroundings of those they advise and help senior individuals have the information and interpretation they need to better judge the future, the present, and for characterizing or extracting whatever is useful from the past.

Let us briefly examine these five categories of information CEOs and top managers need daily from the Trusted Strategic Advisor.

Data

Data is about a sense of the market, a sense of the acceptability of the organization's goods and services. It could be financial, but it is more the metrics of softer things like positive versus negative acceptance, probability data, market velocity data, or failure data.

Perception Analysis

Perception Analysis of various aspects of the business, for example, the temperament of investors. What are they feeling? What are they saying? What are they telling other investors and analysts? What is the emotional state of the organization? What are our people saying? How are they behaving? Are we a happy ship, is everyone having fun? Or is there a feeling of dread, doom, simply rearranging the deck chairs on a daily basis?

Gossip

CEOs absolutely love gossip. Part of it is due to the fact that they are out of the loop with so much that goes on day to day in any organization, including their own leadership group. Another part is the fact that the scuttlebutt is often an indicator to the practiced eye of deeper issues or questions they need to point out to the management team. The things management has only briefly thought and talked about out loud get into the pipeline easily and seem to go everywhere quickly.

Grapevines usually have extraordinary accuracy and move with better average velocity than any formal communications program. Early in his career, while the Cold War was still underway and before the Internet and email, Fred was communications head for an investment bank that was then called First Boston Corporation. He quickly discovered that the best source of information about what was actually happening at the bank was the grapevine. But people at the bank called it "Radio Free First Boston," a riff on the US radio network, Radio Free Europe, beaming accurate information to people behind the Iron Curtain. And Fred used the fruits of Radio Free First Boston to help his bosses stay current on concerns, challenges, and opportunities.

The perceptions senior leaders have of what people are supposing, imagining, and hypothesizing are important in judging the organization's understanding of the key destinations the leader is asking everyone move toward.

What to Do Next

Typically, if you deliver the feedback CEOs need daily, almost immediately you will be asked a series of questions. The questions go something like this:

- What is your take on this information?
- What sorts of new problems, landmines, and potholes are out there relative to what we knew last week?

- What kinds of things should we be thinking about working through to resolve some of the issues this feedback tends to indicate?
- Are there any immediate actions I need to take, or information I need to further develop, to help us stay ahead of what is coming into the organization or moving through the pipe?
- What are the three most crucial answers you need today?

People Assessments

Almost every CEO or leading manager asks their advisors to evaluate those around them. This will include insiders as well as outsiders. Be ready with productive, constructive comments.

Too often, we see internal advisors step back from this responsibility and, while often eager to criticize those who are outside the organization, only speak with great reluctance about those inside. Outside consultants are always asked to rate everyone.

Remember the number two responsibility of all people in leadership positions is to have in place the people and skills necessary to achieve the goals and objectives the boss promised to accomplish. The Trusted Strategic Advisor wants, always, to be in a position to make appropriate comments about everyone else on the team. Having a management perspective requires that the advisor pay attention to what everyone contributes, the nature of what is contributed, and how those contributions can be improved. Be prepared to judge the capabilities and competencies of those in the leader's vicinity and always the leader directly. All outside advisors can count on being asked to evaluate all inside experts and advisors. Be ready.

What Your Leader Expects

Larry Bossidy, former Vice Chairmen of General Electric and CEO of Allied Signal, wrote an amazing article in the *Harvard Business Review* called "What Your Leader Expects of You, and What You Should Expect in Return."[1] Although his article was aimed toward other operating executives who work around CEOs, it contains a very instructive checklist that is highly relevant to the Trusted Strategic Advisor.

Bossidy's approach is timeless and provides a thoughtful and insightful guide for those who advise leaders, just as it is for those who are leaders. Each of these suggestions helps engage the individual in activities that bring productive leadership exposure and experience. These activities, carried out by a strategic advisor, where possible, broaden and deepen the advisor's ability to develop more operationally effective advice.

Do You Have the Discipline?

As should be apparent by now, maximizing your impact means truly focusing on what really matters. This approach is what will help you gain and keep the confidence of senior leaders. Resist joining in with the typical staff complaints about senior management's weaknesses and blind spots, avoid falling back into staff talk, use the boss's time effectively, and carefully structure your verbal recommendation presentations.

As you contemplate what is expected of you, ask yourself some hard personal questions. These questions, candidly asked, will help you develop a productive level of personal discipline and intensity and anticipate, even trigger, the kinds of questions that build your relationship with those you advise:

- Where necessary, how will you fill management's blind spots and suggest ways to overcome management's limitations?
- How do you separate yourself from your own predispositions, assumptions, and anti-management biases?
- What habits do you have that add positive energy to what management has to accomplish?
- How skilled are you at moving different constituencies to listen and act?
- What is your personal strategy for building the expectation of a strategic contribution from you, in management's eyes?
- Can you discipline yourself to regularly use the Three Minute Drill format (see Chapter 9)?
- How will you manage your personal ego involvement throughout the process?

These are tough questions for most of us because we naturally focus on our own needs ahead of management's. When we develop the discipline to focus on management's needs first and foremost, we simultaneously maximize our potential impact on management. They notice.

PART II

The Seven Disciplines

4 Be Trustworthy

Chapter Outline

Trust is the foundation for a relationship between advisor and leader. Learn the five components of trust, five behaviors to establish trust, and 10 ways to lose trust.

Trust Matters

Trust has various definitions like reliability, confidence, and credibility: "you can count on the performance or behavior or thinking of an individual."

Jim's definition, though, is that trust is simply the absence of fear. Fear is corrosive, negative, detrimental, and sometimes toxic to relationships. The feeling of concern that fear generates may cause the boss or leader to ignore, preempt, suspect, or resent the ideas of others, even ideas from advisors who, historically, have had access and credibility. When trust is lost, suspended, or damaged, the managerial attitude of distance readjusts quickly.

As you move up in authority, responsibility, and power, trust is the crucial factor because this ingredient in the relationship is what permits, sanctions, and protects interpersonal openness, candor, truthfulness, and face-to-face engagement. The stakes are always high in the relationship dynamics between trusted advisors and the leaders who rely on them. Serious ideas, issues, or money, even the future, are always on the table. There is also a sense that develops at senior executive altitude that, "Either you're with me, or you're someplace else." Neutral ground is hard to find at the altitude of senior executives. An environment of trust helps to constructively channel emotions and thinking.

Trust is one of the important reasons people are promoted. Sometimes trust has more weight than actual competence or accomplishment. Many senior executives we have worked with have selected surprising people as true confidants. These trusted individuals may or may not have relevant business experience. But, somehow, the boss has come to rely on the judgment, observation, or insight these people provide. It also helps if the trusted individuals pose no particular threat, even when they challenge the most cherished beliefs or inclinations of leaders. Know who those confidants are.

Loss of trust is one of the unstated but real reasons people are demoted, fired, or just ignored at every level. Why? Generally, the higher the altitude in management, the lower the tolerance for mistakes in judgment. Apparent attempts to usurp power to which one is not entitled, and the exercise of authority without support from another leader or established internal benefactor, gets a negative reception. One is tempted to call this politics. Politics certainly is a useful analogy at senior levels. Because to be trusted, especially during times of stress and change, requires the advisor's ability to manage the politics of relationships, including among those around senior leaders.

It is worth noting that most managers and leaders rely on their advisors to develop the necessary relationships among the other managers and executives surrounding them, so the advisor's ideas can be well thought of rather than being designed just to please the manager or boss.

One chief executive mentioned that more often than not, she has had to caution an advisor that pleasing her, while important, was only one ingredient in successfully advising at the upper levels of management. The advisor was expected to build relationships with the chief financial officer, legal counsel, strategic leaders, and the handful of other top people who advise the senior executive. It is the rare consultant who can work exclusively for the CEO and survive for any length of time while ignoring the concerns, issues, questions, and relationships of those also near the top.

An advisor is trustworthy because they are helping and advising, obviously for the benefit of the other person. From the trusted advisor's perspective, it must always be about the other person. One general axiom of relationship success is often stated in terms like, "When you help others get what they want, they will help you get what you want." This is absolutely true in the business of strategic consulting and advice giving. Fail to help, waste time, misjudge your relationship, seem self-serving, or exploit your proximity to power, and the relationship of trust will suffer, or you earn the negative attention of those also needing to have influence over other people.

A question we often hear, especially from more junior aspiring advisors, is, "How old do you need to be to be heard and trusted, or just get in the room?" There are, in fact, many examples in the business world, in academia, in key professions, and in government indicating that competence, expertise, and the ability to convey critical information effectively matter more than age.

Some examples are:

- Steve Jobs (he started Apple at age 21)
- Bill Gates (Microsoft became an independent company when Mr. Gates was 21)
- Warren Buffet (he taught a night class at the University of Nebraska, "Investment Principles," at age 21)

Having spent some time in government service and much more time in the private sector, Jim can tell you that being trusted and being effective are rarely about age. Being trusted, at least at first, is about service to others based on some specific, unique knowledge or aptitude. It's about demonstrating competence even if the area of knowledge is narrow. In fact, the truly general business expert is a rare commodity. Most expert advisors have a limited spectrum of knowledge and experience. What makes them successful is the ability to use their expertise as a platform to have maximum management impact.

One of the great services that the Trusted Strategic Advisor can provide is being alert to future expertise to recommend to those in charge. Just as the CEO has learned to avoid being the know-it-all, so to the Trusted Strategic

Advisor is a scout for talent inside and outside the client organization. We've commented before on the protective nature of staff; the thing to remember is that unlike staff people the Chief Executive working with a very senior operator will have a full horizon of interests that often get activated when challenging situations arise.

If you are around long enough, you begin to recognize that CEOs have enormous reach and an even larger curiosity. It's helpful for you to know whom they reach out to even for the most mundane kind of advice. This matters because your willingness to share other sources with them builds trust even more so at emergent times where it's the boss's neck that is on the line and probably nobody else's.

The more trust you build, the more influence you have, the more access you get, the more acceptance comes automatically. Your behaviors and input provide enormous impact and calmness at serious times. The bottom line is you'll be included in more things and your level of respect among even competitive staff members will grow.

During urgent situations, the younger the executive, the more likely they will feel that they pretty much know how to handle things. Sometimes you find the same situation among more senior executives. Because of really deep experience, we can almost always pull a story or two out, on the spot that will calm things down, maybe entertain ever so slightly, and the boss gets the message that there are better ways and better times to do what has to be done.

Fred began giving advice to clients when he was 23. At age 30, a couple of years after Jim became his mentor, he advised his first Fortune 500 CEO. That CEO, who was in his late 60s, was trying to fend off a hostile takeover attempt. Fred and the CEO spent hours together, preparing him to face skeptical investors, the news media, and other key stakeholders. After the threatened takeover was successfully blocked and shareholders expressed continued support for the company's leadership, the CEO invited Fred to his Park Avenue, New York office to have a celebratory drink.

Afterward, as the two walked through the wood-paneled hallway to the elevator, the CEO put his arm around Fred's shoulder and again thanked Fred for his help. Then he asked, "Oh, by the way, I've been meaning to ask you something. How old are you?" Fred replied, "I'm 30 years old." The CEO stopped in his tracks. His facial expression was a mix of horror and confusion. How could he have put his reputation and his company's fortunes in the hands of someone so young? But he quickly recovered from his initial shock, and they resumed their walk to the elevator.

The answer to the age question is, "It's about what you know and what comes out of your mouth rather than the grayness or absence of your hair," or for that matter, your years of experience.

If anything, continuous and relentless expansion of knowledge, especially in developed cultures and societies, means younger people absolutely know a lot more than someone more senior knew at the same age.

Each generation is better informed and pushing upward faster with a more strategic value in its knowledge base. The greatest challenge for the rising star is building the trust component of their relationships. Too often, it appears that up-and-comers are more interested in their own career trajectory than the crucial tasks managers must meet or accomplish. Remember, when it comes to those you advise, it's always about them, at least first.

Trust and Influence

Having influence means that when the advisor speaks, recommends, challenges, or teaches, decisions will be affected in almost every case. Sometimes, just a look between the trusted advisor and the powerful person is enough to change the flow of events or decisions. Real influence is built incrementally over a longer period of time, mostly by the advisor.

Actually, the benefit of having influence is that those around you, those below you, and even those above you recognize that you have this special ingredient in your relationships with those you are advising. Influence over important individuals and events can have a very interesting and serious level of risk attached to it. Those around you, who may not be trusted, or who have their own agendas or access problems, will come to see you as a potential conduit to influence those you advise.

Influence always attracts the attention and focus of those further away from the centers of power. Another interesting aspect of working at very high altitudes with access to unique and unlimited information is that you become mindful of the proliferation of agendas being worked around those who make the most important decisions. Influence and access attract the attention of those who don't have either. A Trusted Strategic Advisor has to be able to manage the internal politics of access that inherently exist at senior levels. And, there is always politics up there.

Trust and Loyalty

Trust, influence, and loyalty are linked. Trust is the basis for access; access facilitates influence; influence over others often is possible in exchange for loyalty. These ingredients in the advisor's relationships create the perception of loyalty in the minds of those being advised. Loyalty matters at senior levels, and any level of management, because the number of followers matters. The ability to affect change and progress depends on the loyalty of individuals near the top and at many other levels of the organization.

There was a scene on the early 2000s NBC television series *The West Wing* about White House staff people, where one of the president's senior staffers was about to suffer a huge public embarrassment, possibly leading to his resignation or termination. In this environment, like many similar environments in large organizations, when those who are important have big problems, or are even rumored to have big problems, it is customary for colleagues nearby to step away and leave the afflicted individuals to fend for themselves, either rising or falling based on their own actions and responses, or past deeds.

In this scene, Leo McGarry, the Presidents' Chief of Staff, meets with and tells this key individual a powerful story, "A man is walking along and falls in a great big hole. After he picks himself up and figures out what happened, he realizes he's trapped, and he starts to shout for help. A few minutes later, a workman walks by and hearing the man's shouts, looks into the hole and makes a couple suggestions about how he might dig his way out or climb his way out. A little while later, a young woman comes by, looks in the hole, and says she will find some help and call 911. More time goes by and a priest, hearing the man's shouts, looks into the hole and writes a prayer on a piece of paper, then drops it in the hole to console the man. Then, a long-time friend walks by, looks in the hole, hears his friend's shouts, and jumps in. The man in the hole looks at his friend and says, 'Now look what you've done, we're both stuck here.' His friend looks him in the eye and responds, 'Actually, I've been here before, and I know the way out.'"

The final McGarry remark is the punch line on the story. He then said to his friend, "As long as I have a job, you have a job."[1]

This is an example of how trust fosters loyalty and loyalty turns out to be the glue that holds the trusted relationships together, even when there's trouble.

Establishing trust in the first place is the tough part. It is by far easier to recognize those behaviors, behavior patterns, and attitudes that damage trust and personal credibility. Put in a more interesting way, trust, like loyalty, is fragile and magical. Both are products of good relationships.

Jim loves Fred's story. Quite often Jim uses it when people try to figure out what it is he actually does. He's the guy who jumps in the hole and helps the afflicted individual or people find a way out. It's a very powerful story and can be used in many ways to help moderate intentions and expectations and have this trust-building effect for the future. It's a story, by the way, that once heard, people will repeat often elsewhere. Maybe once in a while, they will give you credit for it, but otherwise, it's a great story.

Loyalty Has Limits

In the case of Trusted Strategic Advisor, the relationship is less about blind loyalty and more about a higher level of objectivity and perspective. The concept of perspective means always remaining at some altitude, some constructive distance to assure that the advice given or taken is truly the most valuable and the most helpful. Being objective can, at times, seem less than loyal. This perception occurs most often when the senior executive is choosing between admitting something, hiding something, deferring something, or otherwise delaying something.

This is where the dilemma is, of course, one of disclosure versus denial, or the confirmation of negative events, decisions, or outcomes versus trying to paint them in some other, better light. Yes, even in most of these circumstances, while the most junior employee in the organization can suggest or recommend the correct course of action, it takes the relationship weight of the trusted advisor, bearing down on this very senior person or group, to generate the impact necessary to get the correct decision made.

The trusted individual is willing to take risks based on that trust, including termination of the relationship, should that be required, in giving the best advice or counsel.

In one of the few times that Jim involuntarily lost a trusted relationship (and was fired), he had been working for a couple of years with a fast-growing technology company in the Southwest. Abruptly, the CEO decided to retire, and a new one was brought in, someone whom Jim had not met before.

Over three or four weeks Jim and the new CEO worked together on a couple of projects, and Jim generally thought they were beginning to put a relationship together. Then he called Jim on a Friday afternoon and asked him to prepare announcements for Monday about laying off approximately 600 to 900 people. As it happened, the company was already growing so rapidly that there were at least 500 to 600 current openings for positions all across the organization.

Over the weekend, Jim drafted a tightly drawn, well thought out page and a half email describing how the company could easily shift many of those slated for departure into the open positions already available and needing occupants. At the time, Jim thought that he was providing the type of service his client was looking for in a trusted advisor.

However, on Monday, Jim received a very short response; it was, in fact, just five words: "You're not on my team." Translation: "You're fired."

What Jim had failed to grasp in this new relationship was that this individual, unlike his predecessor, was brought in to sell the company, not to grow it. Jim simply should have known better, or found out, and paid attention.

Jim admits that he should have asked better questions before he launched forth with his recommendations. It was Jim's fault, and the CEO probably felt he didn't have time to bring him up to speed.

As Jim later reviewed the experience, he spotted several decisions and actions that indicated the outcome a lot earlier.

In the future, when this was a possibility, Jim told the story about himself and what he's failed to see as a way of signaling to the people in charge that this was just another rodeo Jim and Fred have been on before. But also, the value of letting key people into the game.

The end of the story is interesting in that the young CEO who was brought in to get the company ready to sell got a truly huge bonus for getting it done so quickly and apparently so competently. The new owners immediately replaced him with someone whose desire was to grow the business as opposed to doing something else. Ironically, the tech businesses are a pretty small family, and so the incoming CEO and Jim were well-acquainted although they had not actually worked together. Jim did re-establish his relationship and help the company resolve the issues that growth always presents.

Trust-Appreciation Confusion

Many advisors suffer from a sense of confusion in that their advice may be taken, even relied upon, yet there is the feeling that their work is not appreciated, and that their contributions and their presence are undervalued. We hear this from younger, less experienced individuals. They ask, "Why aren't there more expressions of appreciation and acknowledgment?" How can I get them (the boss) to acknowledge my value?

Our first response may seem a little flippant, but it usually goes something like, "If you're in the business of being a trusted advisor for the accolades, recognition, and appreciation it will generate for you, better choose another career direction as quickly as possible, because you'll be waiting a long time."

Being a trusted advisor, for those who aspire to it, is the highest level of professional practice. It is done, frankly, without expectation of appreciation, acknowledgment, or recognition. If you truly advise for the benefit of someone else, you will take satisfaction in helping them achieve their objectives, their goals, and their aspirations. If you're in it purely for yourself, it becomes self-evident rather quickly, and it's more likely that someone who can fill the need as we're describing it here, will actually get the access and have the success that you were hoping for.

This thought is similar to what Jim describes as Face Time Fantasy in Chapter 6. Proximity to power is a false indicator of real value. It's the actions leaders and managers take, based on your advice, that counts. You'll have to do the counting if it really matters to you.

The Ingredients of Trust

Trust involves at least five crucial ingredients. As we define them, you'll note that many of these ideas are also a part of leadership, followership, and the ingredients of relationships:

1. **Candor**

   Truth with an attitude, truth plus insightful and honest perspective, delivered promptly. For example, there are always other perspectives on the same set of circumstances. Candor speeds action and helps clarify situations and more options, more quickly, more carefully, and helpfully.

2. **Credibility**

   Always conferred by others who recognize that your past behavior, track record, and accomplishments warrant it. If you deliver what you promise, you'll get the creds.

3. **Competence**

   One of the definitions of competence we like is: The ability to apply special knowledge, experience, and insight in order to resolve the issues, questions, and problems of others. It means putting the power of your intellect and expertise to work for the goals of another.

4. **Integrity**

   The personal, organizational, or institutional inclination to do the right or most appropriate thing at the first opportunity, or whenever there is a choice or dilemma. A person with integrity is someone you can count on to steer you in the right direction or help you make the morally correct decision, often on the spot, every time.

5. **Loyalty**

   Loyalty means faithfulness, sometimes devoted attachment, and often involves a genuine affection for the individual, a willingness to go anywhere, do most anything, follow the lead given, and to spontaneously speak up for someone and/or their beliefs. It is often assumed that once a bond of trust is established, it is difficult to break. Experience demonstrates that the bond itself is fragile. But a bond of trust, once established, generally makes re-establishing a relationship easier.

Establishing Trust

It is extraordinary how the process of establishing trust is similar in situations and relationships between individuals; between individuals and organizations; between organizations themselves; between organizations and society; even between cultures. Establishing trust is the product of sensible, simple, constructive, and practical steps. It's also been our experience that establishing and maintaining trust is a process, carried out with directness and simplicity. There are five elements in establishing and maintaining trust.

Provide Advance Information—a "Heads Up"—Whenever You Can

Advance information is the first and most important ingredient because its absence has one of the most toxic impacts on relationships. You trust another individual above all else because of their willingness to anticipate those situations that could be negative or threatening.

In the context of senior leaders, it's making certain they have, from you, the information they need to achieve their objectives, or to defend or deflect actions or perceptions that could be detrimental to their success or progress. They expect to be warned of danger, damaging decisions or threats, potential disasters, and disloyalty.

Seek the Leader's Input

Asking for input is the second most powerful ingredient of trust. Those being asked are also receiving a signal of their value to the requester. Taking action without asking or seeking input is considered to be arrogant and unempathetic.

Early in his career, Jim was active in a wide variety of organizations engaged in security issues for companies. In one such organization, all members were Senior Vice Presidents of the Fortune 100 Companies. Several were clients of his.

One afternoon he was contacted by one of the senior security people he didn't know who asked him to come down to the Fontainebleau Hotel in Miami and conduct a briefing on some of the more important security issues of the day. Jim was happy to meet him; he was well known in the security community. Jim asked, "Well, about how long were you planning on my speaking?" He said, "About 20 minutes."

Well, it was a beautiful opportunity, no question, but Jim couldn't resist the comment, "That's a pretty short amount of time to go all the way from New York to Miami Beach." His caller responded, "Well Jim, what would be an ideal time for you to speak?" and Jim said, "I made a number of presentations to your group, and they averaged about three hours each." There was a big pause. The gentleman said, "Well I'm new to the group and the chair of the committee to put this program together. I don't believe I can go back to the committee itself and say I have someone who wants to speak for three hours." So Jim said, "I've been with your group for a number of years, and let me give you the names of five different members that I've worked with over the years and without prompting it, ask them how long they would like me to be on the stage." A couple days later Jim was contacted again. "I'll be doggone." his caller said, "Every one of them said three hours or more if he could get the time." Jim got the gig.

These are wonderful people in doing some of the scariest work you can do in your day job. The talk went very well and when Jim returned to his office, this is a very old story, there were about 15 slips on his desk reflecting phone messages. He immediately became worried; what could he have possibly said?

Luckily, among the messages were two or three people that he knew in the organization, so he called them.

The first man worked for one of the top four auto manufacturers. He said, "Well Jim, I don't know about the rest of the group, but I called you because I think you saved my career." This is a true story. Jim cut to the chase immediately and said, "What did I say?" He said, "Well frankly, when you talked about going to the boss before you started planning for crisis situations and emergencies and asking them what they were more afraid of or concerned about. I've never done that."

He said, "I've been here a long time. I'm usually in the habit of preparing a proposal and then I walk in and have a complete, but short discussion. I tried your way yesterday." Jim said, "So, what was the difference?" "The boss immediately relaxed and said, 'This is the first time you've ever had this kind of a conversation with me and I'm delighted. There are three things that keep me awake at night . . .'"

He said, "I suggested I send him a proposal that focused on the three areas that he was most concerned about."

Later that day, other men that he knew (in those days all top security people were male) each, without having spoken to each other, said the same thing. They had always planned on their own without talking ahead of time with their boss on the issues.

Every one of these 12 people had the same question. What if he says no? Jim's answer was immediate: do something else.

But the questioners persisted. What if this is really crucial to the survival of the company and terribly important. Jim answered with a question: Who's name is on the door, and who is driving the bus? It's their bus. If you want to ride up front, seek their advice first.

Long story, lots of powerful lessons here.

Listen Carefully

Careful listening is driven by the conversation or information that is exchanged, the constructive and open nature and the questions that are asked for clarification, and a real sense that each individual or organization is engaged in the conversations that take place during the relationship. Trust depends on careful listening, in both directions.

Change Your Approach Based on What You Hear

When you change or modify your plans or expectations as a result of listening and input, it further demonstrates that you can be trusted. Active engagement, paying attention, and reflecting what is heard is demonstrated by changing previously announced actions, planned behaviors, and outcomes.

Stay Engaged

Trust maintenance is an ongoing, interactive process. Rather than waiting for others to contact you or maintain the relationship, you call, on your own behalf and in their own best interests, to keep the relationship moving, alive, and essential.

The wise advisor helps leaders recognize that their own ability to establish, maintain, and restore trust rests on these same five actions.

Busting Trust

Trust does seem a bit mysterious. It is far easier to identify the behaviors and attitudes that damage it. Earlier in this chapter, trust was defined as the absence of fear. As you'll note in the circumstances below, fear is quite logically the absence of trust. Fear is what fills the vacuum when trust is questioned, damaged, or destroyed. Here are the most frequent and most easily avoided trust busters:

1. **Arrogance**

   Assuming permission and making decisions unilaterally without important input from key partners.
2. **Broken Promises**

   Trust means each party can rely on the commitments of the other, both implied and explicit. When those commitments are broken without prior notification, understanding, explanation, or warning, the first element of the relationship to suffer is trust. Losing the safety of commitment will call into question most other elements of the relationship.

3. **Chest Beating**

   Unwarranted self-congratulatory, self-validating behavior puts distance between those who want to trust and those who need to be trusted. It's a form of self-deception.

4. **Creating Fear**

   This usually occurs when something you do damages or threatens to damage someone who trusts you through surprise and without their permission or advance knowledge. It's the feeling of unreliability, even betrayal, in the relationship.

5. **Deception**

   Misleading intentionally through omission, commission, negligence, or incompetence creates feelings of separation, distance, and disappointment.

6. **Denial**

   Failing to promptly come forward and acknowledge the circumstances when mistakes and errors in judgment produce negative surprises.

7. **Disparagement**

   Easily identified by negative words and descriptions, "He's uninformed," "They just don't understand," and "They wouldn't listen." Victory is never achieved by disparaging others or blame-shifting. Disparagement, when revealed, damages relationships and creates permanent critics, victims, and future opponents.

8. **Disrespect**

   Even adversaries can trust each other to some extent, provided there is a sense of respect. When the reputation of an individual, product, or organization is minimized, trivialized, or humiliated, there is a sense of uneasiness and discomfort that often leads to frustration, anger, and more negative behavior.

9. **Holding Back**

   The essence of trust is having information or confidence in advance of decisions and circumstances so that no matter what happens, those in the relationship are able to count on the behaviors and attitudes of each other. Deliberately withholding information, support, admiration, cooperation, or collaboration corrodes relationships.

10. Minimizing Danger or the Significance of Events

Using or parroting phrases like, "It's just an isolated incident," characterizing something adverse as "old news," failing to accurately and realistically portray serious problems, faulty thinking, and stupidity leads to mistakes and further errors for which the advisor loses the trust of those relying on them.

How Long Should You Stay?

When your longevity effectiveness becomes an issue, the question we hear most often first is, "How do I get these good people I am loyal to and have helped a long time to again listen to and do what I tell them? Jim, Fred, how do you get these executives and bosses to change their ways? I have been with my leader for many years, I trust her, I like her, and we have worked well together but it's impossible to change her mind on so many things. I think she knows what's right but persists in doing something else. How would you make her change?"

At this point, we usually ask how long the senior advisor has been seeking changes. Many say, "From the day I arrived." Then we ask, "How long ago was that?" "Eons ago," is the response they give with a sigh!

Both Jim and Fred have been senior-level advisors to important people for most of their careers. More than just a staff person or PR guy. As a result, they're in the room for lots of stuff from which staff people, especially in PR and HR, are excluded. We got to see how many advisors succeeded or failed at proposing ideas. We have learned many lessons.

When our inclusion, access, and acceptance are ignored, our inclusion preservation strategy kicks in. Early on Jim's career, he adopted a 10-day rule on proposing or persisting in proposing ideas:

a. If the decision-maker doesn't jump on the proposal immediately, Jim gives it 10 days. Then Jim provides a not-so-subtle reminder.

If there is no response or acknowledgment or resistance, Jim forgets that idea and moves on to another. One thing about creative people is that they waste ideas and actually throw ideas out in the trash, every day. Grab one out of the trash and give it a fresh start. Persistence in the face of intentional silence (their silence is always on purpose) can trigger your banishment in place by being ignored and/or avoided.

b. Way too many senior people build up stacks of persistently proposed and persistently ignored suggestions in the hopes of having some kind of breakthrough . . . which never happens.

c. Senior leaders make decisions on suggestions or ideas almost immediately. These are adults making adult decisions. They are paid to quickly decide everything. And they do. When they see you coming down the hall, and they quickly duck into the first doorway to avoid talking to you, take the hint. Their decision to avoid or not to talk with you is immediate, intentional, and many times irreversible.

d. Too many senior people have stuck around in the belief that over time, change will occur. This is simply a tragically false assumption. It's based on the equally false assumption that if we are good, smart, loyal, and pleasantly persistent, at some point they will start listening to us . . . again. That's one of the times it's important to consider moving on. Once they turn you off the chances of turning your back on are very, very small; often nonexistent.

e. We have worked with countless disappointed truly good people who believed, sadly and falsely, that they will be listened to at some point in the future. Some crisis will befall their leader, and the leader will be forced to turn to the formerly trusted helper for assistance. A fantasy. You should know better than that by now.

What really happens is the leaders end up hiring outsiders, fresh faces, a new team is formed and you're not invited. Some loyal subordinates have spent years waiting. But loyalty has limits that are always controlled by somebody else with more power and position than you.

f. This is the Loyalty exception. There is one situation that demands immediate and decisive action. If the behaviors to be changed are outrageous, unconscionable, questionable, monumentally stupid, borderline illegal, actually illegal, false and hurtful, or abusive you have only one choice. Get out of there as fast as possible. Leaders who behave this way will never change and always try to co-opt or shame you into doing something you can never tell your parent, spouse, or children about.

If you stay despite your good intentions, you become an enabler, a co-conspirator, complicit, and a collaborator. When the behaviors get corrected, which usually involves the departure of the bad actor, you will get the boot too, and you should.

Out of 300 clients in 40+ years of practice Jim has been aware of three true conversions from bad to good. There might have been more. The trouble was there were several instances where a bad guy tried to become a good guy, but nobody would believe it. That person got tossed anyway.

g. Loyalty is always a two-way street. The moment it becomes obvious that you are in the lane to nowhere, as hard as it is, it's time to move on. Too many good people have stayed on for what seemed good reasons but wound up disaffected, disappointed, dissatisfied, and trapped by a false unreturned loyalty. Once this happens, your heart, your gut and a few misguided friends may still tell you, "It will be worth it in the end." It never is. But the feelings of sadness, betrayal, and failure remain forever.

h. When there is avoidance, excuses, doubt, and exclusion, leave. You'll immediately be happier and sleep a lot better that night. You will suddenly become a better parent, partner, friend, or neighbor.

i. Make your life about happiness first, which only you can create for yourself, those you care about, and who care about you.

j. Learn the Driving Force of Leadership: Leadership effectiveness requires that most decisions be made quickly. This is what operators do every day. The last thing they want to do is put a bunch of questions on a shelf in their brain. Experienced managers and leaders decide most everything in a matter of seconds. That's because the questions keep coming requiring prompt responses.

k. Some of us have waited an entire career hoping for some event or miracle that never comes and never was.

For the Trusted Strategic Advisor, this is a list of warning signs, indicators, and potential threats to existing trusted relationships. Watch for them; avoid and prevent or preempt them.

Trust evaporates or diminishes from a mixture of these behaviors. Maintaining a relationship of trust requires constant analysis of the relationship to identify and eliminate negative behaviors, confusion, negative attitudes, and unexpected outcomes. Trust maintenance is a personal commitment to loyalty, and a driven sense of long-term interest in the relationship and in achieving the boss's goals and aspirations.

Trustworthiness Checklist

These questions are based on what you've read in this chapter:

- Do you put the interests of those you advise first?
- Are your values clear, both to yourself and to those you advise?
- Do you live by your values?
- Do you have the competence you advertise?
- Are you always on the boss's team?
- Do you recognize, understand, and care about the boss's goals and aspirations?
- How prepared are you to take the actions necessary to repair the damage once trust is broken?
- How often does your boss take action based on your advice?
- How many times (and how often) have you committed any of the 10 trustbusters? Can you think of other behaviors and attitudes to add to this list?
- What are some ways you can implement the five elements of establishing and maintaining trust in your professional relationships?

5 Become a Verbal Visionary

Chapter Outline

Advisors must have powerful verbal skills. Discover the six opportunities advisors have to provide advice verbally, the verbal skill self-assessment, and the six behaviors and actions of verbal visionaries.

Jack Welch, the late former CEO of General Electric, is an excellent model of a highly verbal executive. His life and work, as described by him and others, provide a rich mixture of both complex and extremely simple but powerful lessons for those of us who are trying to run our organizations and advise others.

In his first book, *Straight from the Gut*,[1] Welch talked about one of his early essential goals as he took over GE, the elimination of a vast mid-level bureaucracy that enveloped anyone with career potential and chained their lives to notebooks under the command and control of various mid-level managers, human resource staffers, and others. Throughout their careers at GE, their experiences, infractions, successes, muddles, and occasional assessment all wound up in these notebooks.

Once chairman, Welch committed to uprooting and removing the huge layer of bureaucracy that was paralyzing GE and holding the company back. He fired more than 100,000 people in his first 10 years as chairman. They called him "Neutron Jack," on the model of the Cold War neutron bomb: The buildings remained intact, but there weren't any people in them. During his last 10 years as chairman, he proceeded to rebuild the company on an entirely different basis. The new GE employed even more people than Welch originally fired, but the new management style was radically different.

Mr. Welch transformed GE in the 1980s and 1990s from a bureaucracy into a far leaner company driven predominantly by a verbal vision and approach. Welch's style is exemplified by a specific area called "The Pit," located in GE's world education headquarters in Crotonville, New York. As he and others described it, every two weeks or so, he would visit The Pit to talk with large groups of managers—face-to-face, voice-to-voice, person-to-person. The only communication aids allowed were note cards. PowerPoint presentations, handouts, and other more typical management communication aids were banned. Welch's goal was to get his managers to talk more about their businesses, challenges, issues, and approaches. He moved them away from elaborate, expensive, glossy-but-superficial communication techniques.

What Jim extrapolated from all of this is that one of the keys to Welch's great success was converting GE from a culture of bureaucratese, where everything is documented and stored, into a verbal culture of real-time decision-making and action. With Welch, your ability to explain yourself, debate, discuss, and decide, pretty much on the spot, was a greater determinant of your continued success than whether or not your notebook was up to date.

This is a profoundly different management approach, which, it would seem, only a very strong leader could execute. This approach brings with it a great insight about management and, therefore, it becomes a discipline of the Trusted Strategic Advisor: The business world, the political world, and the nonprofit world all really run at a verbal velocity. Although we do use manuals, memos, slick media programs, and all kinds of high technology communications tools, it is how we speak and verbally direct each other that get things done. Even in this era of the internet, blog, social media, Teams, Zoom, and AI, it is the conversation between and among people that ultimately drives progress.

The trusted advisor has to be able to engage in fast paced discussion in real time, which requires strong verbal skills, and do so in the territory of the executive, which is the future the boss is steering the organization toward. You need verbal skills and a vision of the future; you need to be what we call a verbal visionary. We'll talk about the verbal skills first and then turn to the visionary aspect.

Advice on the Spot

What sets the external consultant or advisor apart most significantly from the internal advisor is the expectation of cogent, useful advice instantly, often based on some experience but very little information. More typically, with internal consultants, the process is to attend meetings, listen, ask questions, absorb the information, then leave to prepare a presentation, response, or outline of a plan for later discussion with the boss.

The problem with leaving to think about things is, of course, that if the issue requires more urgent attention or the boss is focused on it now, strategic decision-making will continue even if staff members intend to return to provide helpful information after a relatively short period of time.

One of the questions Jim frequently hears is, "Why, when the meeting is over, does an outside advisor get to go into the room with the boss and the lawyers and I, who have worked here for 9 or 10 years, have to make an appointment?"

This ability to give advice on-the-spot is one important reason. In terms of verbal skill, providing advice instantly is among the most crucial of disciplines for the trusted advisor. You can train yourself to do this. One way is the Three-Minute Drill, which we discuss in Chapter 9. And later in this chapter, we'll provide some guidance on assessing your verbal skill.

Verbal skill is where the Trusted Strategic Advisor's real power lies. What happened the last time someone presented a plan to the boss to accomplish something you remember, with a beautiful two-inch-thick notebook, 150 pages, 31 tabs, and 15,000 well-chosen words. Was it actually read? Or did your boss simply put his hand on it, look the proposer in the eye, and say, "Show me what's in here and tell me how it's going to help us achieve our objectives." One powerful outcome of visionary communication is to say less but make what is said more important; to write less but make it sayable, listenable, and brief. It is brevity mixed with refined, concentrated ideas and information that powers up the relationship.

The Advisor's Verbal Toolbox

Leaders lead through their ability to verbalize the future, explain a direction, and describe a destination. The advisor also works in real time to help leaders lead in real time. Ideally the advisor's verbal skills should be models the client can learn from and imitate.

The advisor has six powerful verbal tools:

1. **Facts**

   This means data and authoritative information, developed and delivered appropriately and promptly, verbally.
2. **Stories**

   These are structured verbal examples leaders use, which take audiences through ideas, concepts, problems, or situations vicariously, yet teach lessons, morals, or self-evident truths audiences can use to their benefit.
3. **Questions**

   These are questions the leader can use to help engage others in discussions or conversations that move the organization forward. (It's also helpful to provide suggested answers.)
4. **Comparisons**

   This could be a best practice discussion or, more importantly, sharing your perception of how another leader or leaders handled similar problems from different perspectives.
5. **Recommendations/Options**

   The currency of consulting and counseling is recommendations. Unless the way is absolutely crystal clear, it's often helpful to propose a choice of options ranging from doing nothing, to doing something, to doing something more. Recommending options is a process that keeps clients and consultants engaged with each other.

Recommending a useful series of actions along a timeline allows clients to generate momentum and forward motion.

6. **Constructive Confrontation**

   At senior levels, ideas and recommendations are first debated and confronted before any consensus or collaboration process is considered. Be prepared to challenge thinking, ideas, and concepts. The ability to constructively confront, argue, and debate are key expectations of most operational leaders. Just as lawyers are trained to be adversarial, operations executives are trained to decide only after a robust confrontation of all the options.

Be ready to rumble. Managers and leaders are taught that the way to get the best ideas is often through highly confrontative tough language and argument. Be ready. Get coaching if you need it but recognize that on really important decisions the boss is going to let the debate rage for some time until emotions are exhausted, a few key ideas survive, along with their sponsors and advocates, and one or two key concepts or directions tend to emerge.

For many trusted advisors, this is the toughest test of all. Most staff advisors, whether from the inside or the outside, tend to be peacemakers, consensus builders, and direction seekers and momentum generators. Get ready to rumble; get ready to roar. Most senior managers are trained to use this technique because it reflects what was expected of them.

Assess Your Verbal Skill

If you or your company can afford it, and perhaps even if you can't, it is useful, helpful, and sometimes essential to have someone assess your verbal skill. Coaches by the hundreds, perhaps thousands, are available to do this. Let us suggest a very simple internal method to begin with. You can make it more elaborate thereafter if you feel it's necessary.

Install a dictation app on your phone. Get in the habit of turning the app on in meetings. You'll need to tell people you are doing this. Either alone or with someone you trust and respect, go back over these recordings and listen carefully to your conversations. Initially you may be put off by the sound of your voice or surprised by hearing yourself in the context of a complete conversation. The goal is to look for speech patterns and vocal habits that spread confusion or get in the way of solutions and understanding or the truth.

Using this technique is private. You make these recordings only for your own personal benefit, and presumably erase them for continuous reuse in the recording app. Initially it may inhibit conversation, but if you do this consistently it will become a part of what you do in the eyes of others, especially if you report on the progress you are making and what you are learning about yourself.

Another option is to record meetings where you make presentations. These presentations can be transcribed and sent to other managers. You use the recordings to critique your performance.

You will become more discerning about what you talk about and how you say things. If you listen carefully, one of the great revelations will be why people misunderstand you or do things differently than you expect based on the instructions you thought you gave.

In our experience, when this approach is used carefully and continuously, verbal skills improve noticeably. People will notice and comment about it. During Jim's lectures, he estimates that fewer than one in 100 actually take this suggestion and carry it out, but many of those who do contact Jim to talk about how powerfully they were helped by this process.

One CEO's administrative assistant told Jim she had to browbeat her CEO for months to begin doing this. Her boss finally gave in and took one of these devices to his Friday direct reports meeting. As he told Jim afterwards, these meetings always produced additional meetings as a result of the subjects covered. They were held early on Fridays so that everything could be wrapped up before the weekend. This way, Mondays will begin with a fresh perspective, plan, and action—pretty smart.

The CEO related to Jim that within 35 minutes after the meeting ended, three people made appointments to meet with him on Monday. He said that as soon as he saw the appointments on his calendar, he knew exactly why they were there. During the meeting the CEO had told one of the people who had offered a suggestion, that he "didn't think the idea was workable." As the CEO thought about it afterwards, it was obvious to him that these individuals had scheduled meetings to "find out what the heck I was talking about." The CEO knew his comments were unintelligible and confusing.

Regularly listen to yourself talk. This is part of the discipline of verbal skill. You will improve; you will maintain a better sense of on-the-spot verbal planning as you talk. But most importantly, those around you will benefit from your clearer, more concise and constructive conversation.

Get Coaching

If your problems are more serious, you are apprehensive or fearful, or those you respect have suggested that you need help in this area, there are many good coaches who can assist you. Most public relations firms have individuals who are skilled in coaching for public performance and news interviews. You can pick up almost any current book on speaking skills and benefit from one or two, maybe more, ideas that will immediately stand out and you can implement. But the most successful way of all beyond the self-assessment is to locate and use a presentation coach to help you develop and enhance your verbal skill.

Our favorite presentation skills books of all time are *The New Articulate Executive: Learn to Look, Act, and Sound Like a Leader*, by Granville N. Toogood (McGraw-Hill, 2017); and *The Quick and Easy Way to Effective Speaking by Dale and Dorothy Carnegie (1990).* Yes, they have been around a while, but they are simply excellent.

More recent books include *Public Speaking: From Competent to Captivating* by David Gugenheim (Abyssal Publications, 2023); *Talk Like a TED* by Carmine Gallo (St. Martin's Griffin, 2015); and *Think Faster, Talk Smarter: How to Speak Successfully When You're Put on the Spot* by Matt Abrams (Simon Element, 2023).

Being Visionary

The greatest responsibility of leadership is identifying the vision or destinations toward which the organization is moving. The ability to do this is part of the genius all leaders must bring. Some are better at it than others, but all have to have a larger sense of where we are going than anyone else in the organization.

The Trusted Strategic Advisor is a crucial partner in that visualization of an organization's destiny. The advisor's ability to help formulate, organize, structure, and then verbalize this vision is extraordinarily valuable.

Let's delve into this concept of vision, being a visionary, and tie the two concepts together. Jim defines vision as a meaningful, useful, positive goal that many can willingly contribute to achieving. When corporate vision programs fail to reflect this definition, people ignore them because vague visions are simply irrelevant. They often are framed in rigid jargon-driven concepts like "sense of urgency," "hyper effectiveness," or "beyond wow." Even the boss fails to follow them. This is why many corporate vision statements are just nice plaques that hang on the wall.

A visionary is an optimistic individual who can get others to focus on the future, or some meaningful, useful, positive goals, which they willingly contribute to achieving. A verbal visionary is someone capable of moving leaders through sensibly applied speech power, focus on the future and the ability to interpret their vision in ways that energize, mobilize, and inspire.

A true verbal visionary is also quite strategic. A strategist is one who is able to analyze effectively, forecast pragmatically, focus realistically on issues and problems, interpret events and ideas and their impact candidly, and generate ethically and morally appropriate options for decision-making, action, and progress. All top executives are the key strategists in their organization.

Very few managers or senior executives are verbal visionaries. Some will resist the notion of being visionary because they feel their approaches are, at the very least, pragmatic and useful. They may want to resist overstating their face value. A non-visionary is someone who follows rigid rules, someone who is so emotionally attached to personal concepts and ideas that they can't possibly adapt what they are doing to the needs of others. A non-visionary has little tolerance for anything outside the patterns of their own beliefs; they test suggestions and new ideas against their own consistency, the past, and their view of existing culture. Their view of vision accomplishment is more focused on getting "stuff" done, rather than achieving strategies that might yield larger results.

Verbal Visionaries Understand What People Value

A verbal visionary understands people and what people value. Values, in our experience, are protective personal beliefs. Personal core values are almost impossible to change because they serve as such a powerful personal protective mechanism. We're talking about health and safety issues, environmental issues, quality of life issues, work and employment issues, and truly personal values like honesty and integrity. This may well be the opposite of how conventional corporate values are understood, which is why they fail.

Organizations avoid imposing a value system on people; people bring their values into the organization. Wherever these value systems agree, there will be values-driven behavior. Where these values conflict, it is the individual's values, in other words, personal protected beliefs that will prevail and determine behavior and results.

Values exist, individually, person-by-person. Just look around and listen to what people are concerned about, want to protect, or want protection from. By the way, these are the true values of any organization. You can spend a lot of time PRing vision and values and mission documents, but if they don't directly relate to the personal protective beliefs of the people directly affected, they are worthless and, in fact, cause people to distrust those who promulgate such ideas in writing or in words. When bosses and businesses try to change behavior using values-related concepts, hold on to your wallet, especially if the approach is fuzzy, flowery, and obviously meant to substantially change what people already believe. People's values dominate.

A Verbal Visionary Is a Trustworthy Person

Remember, trust is the absence of fear. You trust someone because you feel safe around them. They won't hurt you or are unlikely to hurt you. A trustworthy person has all the attributes discussed in the previous chapter: candor, credibility, empathy, integrity, and loyalty.

A Verbal Visionary Has Judgment

So, we now know that a verbal visionary is a person who is trustworthy; a person with integrity, credibility, and a personal set of values and principles; and, in fact, someone with these habits who is likely to have better judgment than the staff person who just blurts out ideas.

Jim was talking about judgment with a group of senior staffers recently. Afterward, someone sent him a note with a little story explaining how one learns to have good judgment. It's a story about a man speaking to a wise rabbi. The man asks, "How did you become such a wise man?" The rabbi responds, "Study and hard work." The man asks, "What did you study?" to which the rabbi responded, "A lot of my personal experiences." The man then asks, "How did you get a lot of experience?" The rabbi responded, "I have good judgment." The man then asked, "How did you get good judgment?" The rabbi replied, "A lot of bad experiences." Yes, having had bad experiences is a useful prerequisite to being a leader and being an insightful visionary.

Or as the British Prime Minister Winston Churchill was said to observe, "Good judgment is often the result of experience, and experience is often the result of poor judgment."

What Does a Verbal Visionary Do?

Be a Counselor

First of all, a verbal visionary is a counselor: An effective counselor is a pragmatist, a truth seeker and candid truth teller, a storyteller, and an inspiration and motivator to others. As a pragmatist, the verbal visionary defines reality by what will actually happen. In some ways you could say that a pragmatist is the opposite of a dreamer. Most pragmatists have the sense of reality necessary to help bring dreams to life. A pragmatist is someone who gets the getable, knows the knowable, does the doable, and achieves the achievable.

A counselor is a truth coach—someone who avoids the trap of believing in narrow truths that ultimately satisfy no one. If truth seems difficult to find, the counselor helps build bridges to that truth, the whole truth.

Truth is complex. Truth is based on facts interpreted differently by viewers, victims, and participants based on their individual points of reference and emotions. For example, let's say four individuals witness a car accident at an intersection, each from a different corner. An experienced traffic officer interviews these four witnesses. Two witnesses agree on the number of vehicles involved, the other two do not. A different pair agrees on the weather conditions, the other two have different views. A different pair agrees on the condition of the traffic signal at the intersection, the other two disagree . . . After that, all their observations conflict. Why? It is because each individual witnessed the accident from a different point of reference.

Yet, the underlying conflicting information presented by each witness is the truth as they saw it. That's why truth can be complicated. Truth requires understanding and interpretation. Truth requires recognition of the viewer's point of reference. In Jim's view, it is helpful to define truth as 15% fact and 85% perception and emotion. The visionary counselor helps illuminate various points of reference so that the truth, and the various perspectives that truth represents, can be more clearly understood. The powerful insight about truth is that it is generally defined by point of reference.

A verbal visionary is usually very candid. Candor is truth told immediately with an attitude. It is truth with meaning and with insight. A person who is candid is a person who demystifies, who decodes, who deciphers, who de-emotionalizes, and who demythologizes complex ideas and truths. A verbal visionary candidly interprets and clarifies information in ways that are obviously helpful and avoids being self-serving.

Be a Storyteller

A counselor is also a storyteller, and storytelling is among the most powerful verbal techniques in any culture, especially for leaders. The screen and television writer Aaron Sorkin (*A Few Good Men, The West Wing*) says that story is the single most powerful delivery mechanism for an idea ever invented.

Even very experienced communicators often have trouble telling stories effectively. Understanding why stories are so powerful is very important. Stories are one of the verbal visionary's most powerful tools, as they are for leaders as well.

Successful stories are generally told in plain language. They are fundamentally positive. They are about people, animals, living systems, or some combination of the three. They are relatively brief and have a recognizable beginning, middle, and end. Most importantly, stories have a moral, a lesson, what we call a self-evident truth or reason for being told that is immediately recognizable to the listener. Stories help us learn from our own perspective, our own point of reference. We are motivated by the stories of others, but from our own individual perspectives. Each of us can be changed by the same story but in different ways.

Stories also trigger neurotransmitters in the listeners' brains. These include dopamine, the neurotransmitter of both drive and reward, which also has an effect on memory, helping us remember more vividly. And cortisol, which causes feelings of anxiety or even dread. And oxytocin, the so-called love hormone, that relieves anxiety and leaves us feeling even better than before the story began. It is these neurotransmitters that help audiences connect more easily through stories than through dry explanations. These neurotransmitters also help audiences remember the lessons better than they otherwise would.

There are all kinds of stories: stories that make you cry, stories that you make you laugh, stories that make you think, stories that grab your belly and squeeze it, stories that humiliate or make you feel ashamed.

Stories are powerful because they answer the questions we would ask, if we could, about experience: What happened? What was it like? How did it feel? Often it is the opportunity to obtain answers to important questions that draws us to a storyteller, or to a verbal visionary. Stories often clarify the confusion of our struggles and the chaos of daily life. Stories are powerful because they move people. Even the stories that move people to tears, or shame, fear or deeper understanding exert amazing motivational and emotional power. Those who tell stories have great impact.

Every manager needs to use stories as one of their principal teaching, coaching, and disciplinary tools. Readers Digest can help you do that. Readers Digest, first published in 1922, publishes 10 issues per year and is available online (https://www.rd.com). It includes carefully edited summaries of books and lighthearted articles on a range of topics. For decades Jim's mother-in-law began sending him the Readers Digest magazine every month. Jim loved that magazine because it was full of stories that virtually anyone could understand, learn from, or tell. Here's an example.

Jim was going to speak before a large audience of government communicators and was hunting for a relevant story. Jim was once a government communicator himself, which they all knew, so Jim had a bit of latitude about the kind of story I could tell. He came across a story in Readers Digest that was absolutely perfect. It talked about both government communication and working for government.

Here's the story. A man was sitting on his porch on a warm sunny day, looking down the street and watching a city street crew working on the boulevards in front of houses. The truck would pull up in front of each lot, the passenger would hop out and dig a hole in the boulevard and get back in the truck. A couple of minutes would pass and then the driver would get out, fill in the hole, pat the dirt down, get back in the truck, and drive on to the next house. This behavior, of course, puzzled the observer. When they got to his front yard, he hopped off the porch, walked down to the truck, banged on the window, and asked what these guys were doing. The driver rolled down the window and said, "We're planting trees." The neighbor asked, "What do you mean planting trees? Your buddy gets out and digs a hole, then you get out of truck and fill it in, and you drive on to the next house. Where are the trees you're planting?" "Oh," said the driver, "the guy who actually plants trees is out sick today."

Jim's question to the audience was, "How many holes are being dug in your office today because you're at this meeting listening to me?"

Stories are powerful, interesting, emotional, fear-driving, and educational. Yes, stories can also be used to deceive. And they are usually very memorable, which brings me to my next point.

Be Memorable

A verbal visionary is someone who is intentionally memorable. Being memorable is a skill you need to learn. Take the time. Invest in the effort. Being memorable is the key to being a verbal visionary. Being memorable is up to you. No one else will remember unless you make them remember. If they fail to remember you, you're wasting their time.

What does it mean to be intentionally memorable? One example is verbally shaping ideas so as to be easily quoted by others. One test of your memorability is being quoted by others. Do people quote you? Talk in memorable language. Reflect your own sense of destiny to the sense of destiny of those you want to help.

Being intentionally memorable means telling stories well enough so that your stories are carried on and told by others, often without any attribution to you. Your stories are so useful, so helpful, so illustrative, or so interesting that the people who hear your stories will simply adopt them as a part of their own behavior and influence pattern. Use stories that help define how others achieve their objectives.

To be memorable, you have to want to be memorable and you have to do or say memorable things.

Be Inspirational

A verbal visionary is also a motivator and an inspiration. Quite often helping leaders be inspirational is one of the expectations of the coach and counselor. How do you inspire? How does one become a motivator? Are there tricks a person can learn to do this? Our answer is simple, but very serious. One becomes an inspiration to others, and a motivator of others, on purpose.

First, you must want to inspire, to motivate. You have to work on behaviors, model your skills, and share what you say in ways that are motivational and inspirational. This is a skill that is learned, must be practiced, and requires that you pay attention to what moves other people and what other people want. You have to want to help others achieve their goals before you achieve yours or, better yet, adopt their goals and aspirations as your own so you'll achieve them together.

The people who are truly good at this are those who truly want to have an impact on others and who really work at being good at it, having an impact—generally a positive impact on other people. The kind of visionary you're likely to be will be reflected in those you see around you, or who themselves are visionaries today, or who have enormous influence on many people. Study what they do; pay attention to how they motivate and how they inspire. One of the best ways to learn how to do this is to have those who are already good at it around you or the leader you serve.

What inspires you? What moves you forward? A powerful, honest personal commitment to others is required. If those around you fail to inspire you or others, it is time to move on and find those who do.

Jim's mother-in-law was probably among the most inspirational people he has known in his entire life. She had this knack of listening to you speak and then coming up with an absolutely perfect response. Jim often felt that she should write a book of her own about the wisdom she has. One time they were talking about another relative who was being given a hard time by both his family and his pastor. Among the other things, this relative had a drinking problem. Ruth's analysis was, "More often than not, you're going to find far greater compassion in a bar than in a church."

Be Thoughtful

A verbal visionary is also thoughtful. A thoughtful person does four critical things routinely.

First, the thoughtful person uses verbal contrast analysis. In other words, when a thoughtful person analyzes a situation, problem, issue, or opportunity, they are able to draw a verbal contrast between good and bad, between bland and colorful, between the emotional and the factual. This is what people are looking for in terms of help. Useful simplification leads to verbal contrasts, which inspire understanding.

Second, a thoughtful person asks good questions. These questions are asked to help build understanding, rather than attack, demean, diminish, minimize, or bully. These are generally open-ended, abstract, and complex questions, not yes-no questions or requests for facts. Good questions generate answers that help everyone within earshot.

Third, a thoughtful person is constructive skeptic. This means that when obviously conclusive evidence is absent, ideas, purposes, and intentions can still be constructively analyzed. Imperfect ideas can be usefully dissected and thoughtfully examined, then discussed—again with a focus on learning, with a focus on illustrating, with a focus on understanding, with a focus on gaining insight. It's triggering insight that really leads to what we perceive as wisdom.

Fourth, a thoughtful person states the obvious at every turn. Stating the obvious simplifies so many things very, very rapidly.

Jim's favorite story about stating the obvious comes from a story sometimes attributed to a Sherlock Holmes novel, *The Hounds of the Baskervilles.* In one scene where Holmes and Watson are tracking a murderer across a Scottish moor, and they are forced to camp out overnight. Early in the morning, Holmes wakes Watson and says, "Watson, Watson, look at those stars. What do they mean?" Watson replies, "Well, Holmes, horologically it's about three o'clock in the morning; meteorologically, it's likely to be a pleasant day; theologically, God is in his heavens and his minions are resting comfortably in their beds. What does it mean to you?" "Watson, you idiot," said Holmes. "Someone has stolen our tent!"[2] A funny, but powerful story.

Being thoughtful can yield the dramatic and positive simplification of complex ideas and concepts, which can snap on that little light in your brain—that powerful, momentary illumination of understanding or insight. Sometimes it's simply the blindingly obvious. You suddenly see what you just couldn't see before. Simplification and focus are important parts of being a verbal visionary.

It is the fundamental truth sometimes referred to as Occam's Razor, after the 14th-century mathematician and philosopher William of Occam. He said (paraphrasing) that the more you shave away the complexity of a problem, assuming most other factors are equal, the simplest explanation is likely to be the correct explanation. It is often also the most sensible explanation.[3] Going there is usually very wise.

Individuals who are thoughtful can be very insightful. To us, a person who is insightful is a person who can extract intuitively clear ideas from existing complex situations or information. We listen to them or read their words, and we feel or we instinctively know that they are right or that what they are saying has inherent value. A person who is insightful opens new doors or pathways by detecting useful information, clarifying misunderstanding, and distilling simplicity from complex ideas and information. An insightful person can creatively illustrate a problem, idea, or issue; develop a quick, concise, and powerful analysis that affects the listener or reader with a sense of relief, surprise, clarity, or closure due to the utter usefulness of the ideas and thinking being shared.

Be Ethical

A verbal visionary is ethical—that is, principled, and a person who lives by a set of rules and personal command behaviors all of us recognize as predominantly in the interest of others. A verbal visionary is an advocate for honorable action, an individual who is morally assertive (minus the religious fervor) with passion for the right behaviors, ideas, and actions at every turn, especially in the face of ethical dilemmas.

Be a Coach and Mentor

A verbal visionary is a coach, someone who is committed to helping others more than helping themself by usefully interpreting events and ideas, by illustrating new approaches, by exemplifying the very behaviors, the ideas, and concepts that will best help the individual being helped. A coach can forecast patterns, predict with a great deal of accuracy how organizations and individuals behave; and is the one who prepares everyone for the unintended consequences of their actions.

A verbal visionary is also a mentor. A mentor is someone who starts from the other person's point of view or reference, always. A mentor is someone who helps others focus on goals that are worth achieving; who helps leaders build followership; a person who helps others see options they can't see for themselves. A mentor is someone who is outcome focused. By that we mean someone who's always focused forward, focused on the future.

These are also key elements in the definition of a strategist. A strategist is someone who is focused on what is going to happen, what can happen, and what the possibilities are; someone who knows the lessons of the past as opposed to someone who is always looking backward;

trying to re-analyze, re-live, re-define, or re-interpret history—the old should've, would've, could've analysis that helps no one, and backs one into yesterday.

How Do You Become a Verbal Visionary?

So how do you begin to become a verbal visionary, or know if you are one already? What are the attributes of a verbal visionary?

Your analysis begins by asking yourself some very difficult but important questions. For example:

- What do you believe? What are the truths of your life? Even though what you believe rarely changes, write it down. Say it out loud. We promise you, this is a surprisingly powerful personal experience.
- Who are you? How do you describe yourself? Say it out loud. Write it down.
- What are your personal limitations? Are there things you can't do or won't do?
- What are your aspirations? Who, what, where do you want to be? Write them down.
- What are your principles? What are the parameters of your life? Write them down.
- What is your daily goal, or reason for doing what you do?
- What is your destiny?
- Do you have an inner sense of where you are going?
- What do you want to leave behind?
- What will people remember about you?
- What do you want people to remember about you? Write it down, in 100 words; say it out loud.

Talk these ideas through. Say them out loud. Get in the habit of asking important questions about yourself. Refine and test your answers against your experience and expectations of yourself. Be prepared to talk about them in the context of those you counsel. Leaders do this automatically. They can usually describe all of these topics because their life experience and expectations are the basis for their leadership.

Another ingredient of the visionary is virtue. What are your virtues, those forces in your life that help you stay focused on achieving useful, important, powerful, and good things? And those personal habits that keep you out of trouble?

One of the most famous lists of virtues was developed by Benjamin Franklin. He wrote about them extensively in *Poor Richard's Almanac*, and his notes and records exist to this day. He began with 12. Each was printed on a separate page in a diary he kept. He would pick one and work on it for a month, then select another, month by month throughout the year. His original 12 virtues were temperance, silence, order, resolution, frugality, industry, sincerity, justice, moderation, cleanliness, tranquility, and chastity.[4] He kept this work, and log, and effort up for more than 50 years. An interesting side story about Franklin's list of virtues was that sometime later in his life, as he became world famous, some of his friends in Philadelphia would remind him that he was becoming a bit insufferable. A couple of them even suggested that he needed to add another virtue to his famous list of 12. That thirteenth virtue was humility. Franklin added it, and worked on it as he did the others.

Consider using Franklin's approach. A verbal visionary lives and works their principles, values, aspirations, virtues, and vision every day. What are your virtues, those personal habits that need to be maintained, cultivated, practiced, and exercised to maintain their impact on your life?

You will find that those who come to rely on you as a verbal visionary will expect you to express and discuss your principles, your aspirations, and the foundation of your beliefs, where your thinking comes from, and how you arrive at your own internal destinations. Anyone can offer advice and guess with no particular basis of fact or knowledge. Being a verbal visionary is understanding your self-concepts deeply and sharing them as a method of reinforcing the value and depth of your advice. This approach to your life helps you guide important people in their lives.

We are talking about a whole new level of personal presence in your ability to explain and discuss your advice, your vision, and the vision you have for others based on your own belief systems, those things that motivate you. It is this ability that builds respect. You have respect when those you advise honor you and hold you and your ideas in high regard. You'll know you are influencing their lives. If you don't feel this, you simply are not doing it. You are, in fact, wasting someone's time.

You also have to strive to understand the beliefs of those who rely on you:

- What do they believe?
- What motivates them?
- What frightens them?
- What are they hoping to achieve?
- How can you help them achieve their objectives?
- What is obviously true?
- What is obviously untrue, silly, naive, or stupid?
- Where or how can you make the most important contribution for those individuals—from their perspective?

Write this information down, too. Then take another step. Contrast your beliefs directly with their beliefs. Contrast what motivates them with what motivates you. Contrast how they believe they can use your help with how you believe you can help them. Contrast what's true to them versus what's true to you. Contrast what's silly to them with what's silly to you. What is the most important contribution you can make to them, from their perspective? Can you make it?

Think of a contrast analysis as a single sheet of paper with a line drawn down the center, from top to bottom. Write your beliefs and aspirations on the left side of the sheet and the boss's aspirations and expectations on the right. Do they match? How different are they? Contrast analysis is a simple, extremely efficient and effective talking, teaching, and personal learning tool.

How Will You Know If You Have Become a Verbal Visionary?

One of the most satisfying and powerful aspects of being a verbal visionary is knowing that the advice you offer and your ability to explore important personal ideas and concepts are genuinely helpful in terms of the other person's goals and objectives, personal beliefs and motivations, sense of reality, and priority of ideas. They tell you, they tell others, and your insights become evident in their decisions, actions, beliefs, and strategies.

Can you sense the power of a verbal visionary? Can you become one? If this concept seems to be "out there" for you, my suggestion is that you rethink just how much you want to be in that inner circle. How much can you actually contribute?

You have role models in your life who can help you refine your verbal visionary skills—memorable people, whether they're relatives, friends, teachers, or famous or not famous people. You remember them predominantly because of what you saw or heard, learned or felt, how they affect you.

Your greatest role model of all may be the leader you counsel or want to counsel, just down the hall.

If you want to take up the challenge of becoming a verbal visionary, here's a personal checklist you can use to assess your progress and practices:

- Do you act and speak in other people's best interests all the time?
- Are you a mentor?
- Can you be outcome-focused?
- Are you quoted by those you respect and those who seek your help?
- Do people take action based on what you say?
- Do people tell you or talk about you as being a person of vision? Or as being a person of extraordinarily positive help?
- Do you feel like a verbal visionary? Can you tell when you're actually moving people to action and helping them find the emotional energy to benefit themselves?
- Can you describe your own sense of destiny, your principles, your beliefs, your limits?
- Can you systematically go after the truth first? Are you a pragmatist?

The more "yes" answers, the more likely it is that you are well on your way to becoming a verbal visionary. The more "yes" answers, the closer you are to being a visionary person.

Navigating Contentious Situations

Often an advisor will get tangled in unpleasant, difficult, and often confrontational situations. In many instances it is because others around the top leader feel threatened and try to discredit or otherwise marginalize the advisor. It is possible to address contentious public circumstances and situations, and behave with integrity, honesty, and even good humor.

If your mother could teach you the rules for winning in the irritating, aggravating, agitating environment of being under attack—personally, politically, or professionally, these are the 27 techniques and practices she (or most moms) would share. You can succeed even in the face of contentious people, even angry neighbors, negative media coverage, and irritated public officials.

This means providing authoritative information, developed and delivered appropriately and promptly, verbally.

1. **Speak only for yourself.**

   Say less, write less, but make these communications truly important.
2. **Answer every question.**

   Aim for 75- to 150-word responses; this is 30–60 seconds reading or speaking time. Honorable organizations, people, programs, and initiatives can answer any question.
3. **Always let others speak for themselves.**

   When you try to speak for others, you will always be wrong and attacked or humiliated for being wrong.
4. **Avoid claiming that you agree with your attacker on anything, unless they say so first.**

   Once opponents say it, you may quote them saying it, but always say what you believe to be true and back that up.
5. **Avoid saying that you work closely with public agencies, other organizations.**

   Avoid also saying you work closely with individuals related to your situation (even if you believe you do), unless they say so first and you then quote them. Otherwise, they can deny it (especially if controversy arises) or point out, as some may quite quickly, that whatever links exist are rather weak. They will then describe those weaknesses or deny that you have any real influence.

   Those who can and may support you in the future (public or private) must have their status preserved for the long run. Drawing them into your discussion could needlessly make them targets of attack. They will have to abandon or, perhaps, denounce or distance themselves from you.

6. **Assume that everyone in the discussion has more credibility than you do.**

   Your job is to validate your credibility, every time, rather than to discredit others.

7. **Be relentlessly positive.**

   Avoid all negative words and be constructive. Avoid criticizing and criticism. Both provide the fuel opponents thrive on.

8. **Focus on the truly important.**

   Forget the rest. Respond to and develop what truly matters.

9. **Let attackers discredit themselves.**

   Their emotional words and negative, destructive language equals less truth and trustworthiness. Avoid "friends" who suggest this approach. It will always backfire.

10. **Practice laggership.**

    Speak second but always have the last word.

11. **Remain calm; be positive.**

    Critics, agitators, and bullies are energized by anger, emotionalism, whininess, and negative counter attacks.

12. **Silence is always toxic to the accused.**

    After a while, even your friends will sacrifice or question you.

13. **Apologies are always in order.**

    Be sure your apology contains all of the crucial ingredients of an effective apology. The most constructive structures for apology are in *The Five Languages of Apology: How to Experience Healing in All Your Relationships,* a book by Gary Chapman and Jennifer Thomas. Here, with some paraphrasing and modification based on our experience, are the ingredients of the perfect apology.

    1. Regret (acknowledgment): A verbal acknowledgment by the perpetrator that their wrongful behavior caused unnecessary pain, suffering, and hurt that identifies, specifically, what action or behavior is responsible for the pain.
    2. Accepting Responsibility (declaration): An unconditional declarative statement by the perpetrator recognizing their wrongful behavior and acknowledging that there is no excuse for the behavior.

3. Restitution (penance): An offer of help or assistance to victims, by the perpetrator; action beyond the words "I'm sorry"; and conduct that assumes the responsibility to make the situation right.
4. Repentance (humility): Language by the perpetrator acknowledging that this behavior caused pain and suffering for which he/she is genuinely sorry; a commitment to do what is necessary to prevent a recurrence of what caused that pain.
5. Direct Forgiveness Request: "I was wrong, I hurt you, and I ask you to forgive me." This is a transfer of power, explicitly giving the person who was harmed the power to choose whether to forgive the person who caused harm. The most difficult and challenging aspects of apologizing are the admission of having done something hurtful, damaging, or wrong, and to request forgiveness.

Skip even one step and you fail.

14. Have courage and refuse to be distracted.

Don't be distracted by negativity, friendly pressure, or the agendas of others. You are in the spotlight. They are in the shadows. Be especially wary of those who feel that responding empowers others, or that you might look weak for having done it. Either of these outcomes is better than being considered boorish, bullying, arrogant, or callous.

15. Discourage others from explaining your situation.

They will get it wrong. You will be blamed, and they will be attacked. They will then have to abandon you altogether, keep some distance, or attack you to preserve their own credibility.

16. Everything that goes around, comes around.

Avoid the words, phrases, arguments, assertions, and statements you write or say that you know you will have to eat sometime in the future.

17. Remember the math of truth.

Truth is 15% facts and data and 85% emotion and perception; Facts do matter, but addressing the emotional component of issues and questions immediately, continuously, and constructively is essential for success.

18. Be strategic.

Say, act, plan, and write with future impact in mind.

19. **Prepare to work alone.**

    Be ready to be abandoned by just about everyone.

20. **Stay at altitude**.

    Keep a distance, avoid taking events or actions personally, and be reasoned, appropriate, and direct. Positive and constructive responses tend to disempower those making the attacks.

21. **Keep testosterosis under control.**

    Every bit of negative energy you throw in their direction will multiply by a factor of five to 10, and they will throw it right back at you.

22. **Be preemptive.**

    Work in real time. Do it now, fix it now, ask it now, correct it now, challenge it now, and answer it now.

23. **Be constructive.**

    Write and speak simply, sensibly, positively, empathetically, and constructively.

24. **Avoid trying to discredit anyone, any argument, any evidence, or any movement.**

    Such actions stimulate the creation of more critics and adversaries who accumulate, hang around, live forever, and search relentlessly to exploit your weaknesses, vulnerabilities, and susceptibilities. Remember, your adversaries have tons of stuff readily available to dump on you should you negatively attack them. They've been watching you for months, perhaps longer, and are prepared to reload and reshoot in a moment of your irritation. Prove your position with positive, declarative language.

25. **Hang in there.**

    Get accustomed to the long-term, relentlessly negative nature of contentious situations.

26. **Correct, clarify, and comment on matters promptly.**

    Correct on your own media platforms. Avoid joining blogs or conversations outside your site. The latter strategy will suck all of your energy into responding to the agendas of others who are having fun and sleeping well, while you are doing neither.

27. **It is your destiny.**

    Fail to manage it, and someone else is waiting in the wings to do it for you.

6 Develop a Management Perspective

Chapter Outline

Management advisors need to talk about the boss's goals and objectives. You need to be able to see the business or organization through the leader's eyes.

Staff functions tend to work as though their recommendations, big ideas, or silver bullets will save the day for management.

In reality, silver bullets, big ideas, and brilliant strategies are extraordinarily rare. Those in operations learn relatively quickly that most progress is actually made incrementally, often following established patterns of thinking, experience, scientific or at least rigorous exploration and study, with a hint of intuition and strategic thinking. Most real solutions arrive by accident and chance, as the by-products of some incremental approach.

The Trusted Strategic Advisor, first and foremost, develops the discipline of understanding management and relying on management points of reference. Before you can be invited into the inner circle, you have to sound like you know things that matter there.

Often people in staff functions assume that when they get to the top of their function they will be automatically admitted into the inner circle. And they are baffled by the realization that they are not. And they sometimes become resentful. It shows.

Fred spends a lot of time with such leaders who assume an entitlement to entry into the inner circle. He tells them the tough news, quoting the late former United States Secretary of State and National Security Advisor, Dr. Henry Kissinger: "In a bureaucratic dispute, the side having no greater argument than their hierarchical right is likely to lose. Leaders listen to advisors whose views they think they need, not those who insist on a hearing because of the organization chart."[1]

So the signal question is: How do you become the advisor whose views the boss thinks they need?

Admission to the Inner Circle

Despite the fact that many senior and top managers are loners, or at the very least, selective about who gets near them, there almost always is an "inner circle." Those who populate this special group can be surprising. The variety can range from a person in the shipping department to the President of the United States. What does the shipping clerk have in common with the president? It's all in the eyes, emotions, and needs of the beholder, the CEO.

One thing these advisors all seem to have in common is the ability to provide the leader with suggestions and options from which the leader can then fashion a solution or process to reach a decision.

An early client of Jim's, we'll call him Armando, was the head of corporate security for one of America's largest companies. He was, in that position, an extraordinarily sought-after advisor to the CEO and senior management. Armando told Jim that when he first joined the company from the FBI he came to the attention of the CEO because he had to be a stand-in for his boss at a social gathering. When the time came for someone to organize the presentations, Armando stepped forward. In the process of carrying out this assignment, he told a couple of stories and, he said with a straight face, he sang a short song. As it turned out, the CEO was quite taken by Armando's extemporaneous ability and began inviting him to other meetings. Armando's stepping forward in this circumstance brought him unexpected, important attention from people who mattered. With what started out as a unique, chance circumstance, he was able to build a career based on powerful relationships with very senior people involving some of the most important issues the corporation was facing, in the United States and globally.

From this early accidental platform, Armando was able to turn his FBI career experience, spent mostly in Central and South America, and his ability with languages, into a formidable asset to the management of this huge global corporation.

While it sounds like a cliché, your mindset has to be about putting yourself into the manager's shoes, both operationally and non-operationally. This, among other things, means being conversant with current business plans, key business strategies, and having some familiarity with the metrics of the business. These make up the boss's world. If you want to be there, get with the terrain. The discipline of management perspective is the discipline of reducing exuberance and instilling a measured, more thoughtful and incremental approach to making recommendations and suggestions.

Familiarity with key or crucial business issues is essential. These are those questions, roadblocks, barriers, and threats that can confound even the most enlightened management and the most aggressive and cohesive organization. If the greatest threat has to do with people's attitudes, get good at understanding these circumstances. If the problems involve markets and marketing strategy, find a way to become more strategic and knowledgeable in these areas. It's these key issues that often derail the most well-thought-out plans. What does keep your boss awake at night? What's left to be done from last week? In many respects, until these issues are addressed, nothing else generally matters.

Define your staff function in management terms rather than just in the terms of staff expertise. Failure to align the activities and goals of a staff function with management objectives is often why the staff person is considered less important to the operations team. Here's an example using the public relations function, although it applies equally well to other functions such as legal, HR, marketing, finance, or IT.

Both Jim and Fred have had numerous conversations with management that all align on these conclusions:

1. PR staff are rarely thought of as having sufficient knowledge or practical experience to contribute operational solutions.
2. PR recommendations can come across as public relations speak dressed up in the business vocabulary of the moment. When the rhetoric is stripped away, there is only communications speak and very few operational solutions.
3. Management has learned the lesson—from PR staff—that it is far easier to take an operating person and make him or her into a public relations or public affairs practitioner than it is to transform a public affairs or public relations practitioner into an effective operating executive.
4. The PR focus is too often on defending the function, the media, even the words "public relations." One frustrated executive told Jim, "I wish they'd be as passionate about the needs I have around here as they are about defining and defending what the news media does and needs."

We're sure you can come up with a similar list of management perceptions about your particular function.

The example we gave in Chapter 3 provides another way to look at using management language. You'll recall that when a communications firm was acquired by a large international consulting firm, they undertook to reinvent the language they used to describe their services. "Internal communications" became "employee loyalty building"; "brainstorming and ideation" became "strategic planning"; "communication audit" became "operational review and analysis"; "crisis management" became "readiness"; and so on.

Notice the much more powerful feelings these descriptions inspire. They also contain words managers tend to understand. The question for communicators is: do they understand the words, and how their activities can be described and carried out from a more management-oriented perspective?

The PR practitioner may resent having to translate professional functions and services, skills, and techniques they care about so deeply into the more turgid language of management. It is simply a practical reality that to be understood by management, translation into management terms is essential, provided the staff expert or outside advisor can actually execute in the management environment.

Paradoxically, PR people are generally good at understanding what matters to the stakeholders they generally interact with. And they embody one of Fred's axioms: You can't move people until you meet them where they are. But when it comes to senior managers, PR people often expect the senior managers to meet the PR people where they are. It never works.

The Perfect Communication Syndrome

Communications and Human Resources suffer similar challenges with management. That's because in terms of managing human beings, very senior people feel awfully confident, in fact, over-confident of their successful approach to accomplishing these tasks.

Communicators always face special challenges because most managers believe that they are good communicators, even perfect communicators. When Fred and Jim are speaking before crowds of our colleagues, we usually ask a question similar to, "How many of you work for a boss who thinks they are a bad communicator?" (Big laugh). If we raise our hand and hold it up in the air, after a few seconds, if there are more than 100 people in the audience, one person will finally raise their hand, which gets even more laughter.

The reality is that from the time an individual becomes a supervisor, they are conscious of the power of their communication and most of them with or without coaching seem to think they are pretty good at it.

Here's the problem, when a boss talks to the accountants or to security or to strategic planning, the boss has a rudimentary knowledge of these areas. But nearly all bosses believe they communicate well. As a result, bosses at every level often don't listen to the advice of their communicators. They're actually going through a mental argument about whatever the communicators say, sometimes they're thinking:

- "Well, I'm smarter than this person."
- "He doesn't know what he's talking about."
- "I can think of better things than this person."
- "Who is this person?"

This kind of internal conversation tends to blank out what the communicator is saying, regardless of its quality. The more senior the person, the more the communicator needs to view the techniques we're talking about in this book to help essentially overcome the distraction that leaders or managers are going through when they are having conversations with communicators.

One of the frequent questions we get from colleagues is, "How did you come to have so much access to senior people?" The answer is that we practice what we're preaching here. Looking at everything from the manager's or advisee's perspective and resisting giving lectures on communications and the news media. In the latter category, many senior people have very active contact with reporters and news organizations. Here again, their direct contacts are more powerful than your indirect contacts.

Most importantly, how you give them advice is critically important. In Chapter 9 we will teach you a very unique strategy called the Three-Minute Drill.

One of the major goals of this book is to teach you how to build your acceptance, your access, your impact, your inclusion, your influence, and respect. Understanding that leaders and up-and-coming leaders learn early to rely on their own communication skills. Advising them requires the kind of special handling we're talking about in these chapters.

Commit Yourself to Management's Team

One of the more challenging issues facing trusted advisors is the realization that to be inside, to be close by, to have that close relationship, you have to do more than just want to be there or feel that your position has some inherent right to be there. You have to take an emotional and psychological leap forward and put yourself as directly as possible into the environment and mentality of this person you are advising. You need to meet that person where they are. How do you do this?

One helpful way is to address a series of professional commitment statements. You can be comfortable with these statements because they help you get to where you need to be and reveal your commitment to understand, support, and work with management from their perspective.

1. Service is why I'm here—to protect, serve, advise, and represent the boss rather than my department or function.

2. It is top management's vision and values that drive the organization's day-to-day, long-term, rather than my personal agenda. Remember, the trusted advisor always focuses on the needs of the person being advised.
3. The coaching process begins by understanding what the boss's problems are. My job is to set my problems aside.
4. My job is to help management solve, control, contain, preempt, and counteract management problems. I'm there to make sure success happens, even if that success makes things difficult for my department. I'll suggest solutions that may be good for the organization even if my function has to take a hit.
5. Building followership is a key strategy and management goal. I am a loyal follower, and I can help build more.
6. Expressing solutions in management language rather than staff language helps top executives feel mentored and motivated. This is one of the key reasons trusted advisors are around—to mentor, motivate, and inspire.
7. Making positive suggestions is a constant goal. I will forgo criticism. Criticism is negative, distracting, and creates enemies and critics.
8. The boss knows and listens to me because I am a professional and a Trusted Strategic Advisor. My work and attitude, and the strength of my advice are the justifications of my value every day.

Ask Managerially Relevant Questions First

One of the most important roles of the Trusted Strategic Advisor is to ask constructive questions that help broaden understanding and move processes and decision-making to the next level.

Too often, staff tends to use questions as a means of murdering, maligning, often even demeaning other advisors and their advice. Here are some examples:

- "Why am I just hearing about this now?"
- "Where is the justification for this request?"
- "Where did this come from?"
- "How many have done it successfully before?"
- "Why wasn't this circulated earlier for more thorough consideration?"
- "Who authorized this much off the reservation effort?"

We often refer to this as death by question. If this is your approach, you need to end it immediately. Insults and needlessly combative negative opposition through questioning are always remembered. What goes around will come back around. Negativity creates critics, victims, and adversaries. These individuals persist forever and resurface at the worst possible times. Avoid this behavior on your own part.

Managerially relevant questions are designed to foster discussion and the productive exploration of ideas. They bring more critically essential understanding to the boss. Here's a list of those kinds of questions, which are almost always relevant:

- How does the current situation affect strategy?
- Which management mistakes change the strategy?
- How can we gain employee commitment to the changing circumstances that are causing the problem we're now facing?
- What strategies are available to us to keep shareholder interest aligned with our goals?
- Can management make the tough decisions and act quickly enough to turn a problem situation into an opportunity or at least into a mitigative circumstance?
- What resources can management allocate now to deal with the issues at hand or to resolve matters in ways that move us toward our strategy?
- What have peer companies, in similar circumstances, done? Do we care?
- How will the present circumstances affect our ability to research and develop new products, services, and ideas?
- Is this a situation that requires adaptation or dramatic shifts and changes?
- What non-financial factors are of greatest concern? What about the direct financial factors?
- Will customer satisfaction be adversely affected?
- What are the compliance and ethical implications of the current situation and what remedial steps will be necessary?
- Have any rules, regulations, or laws been bent, broken, or compromised?

If many of these questions seem confrontational, this is because they are. This is part of your role as a constructive skeptic, as a productive, constructive questioner. It is a part of the rough and tumble world of a top strategic advisor.

Get comfortable asking questions that have a confrontational tone. It's expected. But note that confrontational questions are not expressing criticism, but rather provoking thinking.

Fred has found that asking certain kinds of questions in a certain order can further accelerate management's thinking and understanding. At Fred's firm it is called the Q Cycle: It is a cycle of three categories of question.

Category 1 is asking open-ended, abstract, and complex questions to establish clarity about the problem, opportunity, or challenge being addressed. Examples include:

- Which groups are most important to us in this situation?
- Which risks are most significant here?
- What would successful resolution of this crisis look like?

These kinds of questions help establish a common understanding in both the boss's frame and the advisor's frame of reference. After a round of such open-ended questions, the advisor then moves to the second category.

Category 2 is forcing the boss to choose among alternative interpretations, to prioritize. This helps the boss more accurately understand priorities; to assess the relative weighting of alternatives. Examples include:

- Who is more significant here, our investors or our employees? If the boss says that both are important, the advisor should politely push back. "Yes, but if we had to prioritize: do we prioritize our investors or our employees first?"
- Which risk is more significant here, financial or safety? Again, if the boss says that both matter, the advisor should politely push back. "Yes, but if we have to start with one, do we start with financial risk or with safety risk?"
- In this circumstance, who would be most effective to meet with regulators, you or the general counsel?

This works because it forces the executive to articulate aloud a previously unstated prioritization. This helps to clarify the boss's understanding, to the boss themself, and to the advisor.

The third category of question is to play back or name what was heard and what was not heard, and to ask for confirmation or clarification. Examples include:

- From what I've heard you say the last few minutes, it sounds as if your top priority is to protect the brand. Do I understand that correctly? If the boss says, "Yes, that's correct," you have agreement on a priority. But if the boss says, "Actually, no. Now that you put it that way, I can see that the top priority is to protect public safety. If we do that well, we will protect both our financial condition and our brand." Now you have provoked an original insight; your questioning has caused the boss to think differently about the situation.
- Earlier you said that investors are your top concern, but for the past few minutes you've been speaking only about our employees. And I haven't heard anything yet about customers. Have I missed something?

Very often this naming of what hasn't been said provokes the boss to reprioritize, again provoking the boss to think differently than they would otherwise have done.

And this is a cycle, so it is iterative. After the first round of open-ended questions, forced choice, and playing back, the cycle continues with yet more open-ended questions, forced choice questions, and playing back what was heard and not heard.

Several years ago, Fred used this technique with a client, the division head of a global pharmaceutical company to whom Fred had been a trusted advisor for years. We'll call that executive Kevin. Fred got a call from Kevin's speechwriter saying that Kevin needed Fred to come to the company's headquarters to help Kevin rehearse an important speech. Fred expressed some surprise at this. He had worked with Kevin for years and knew him to be a good speaker. When Fred arrived, the speechwriter was in the conference room with three copies each of the speech, the PowerPoint printouts, and a PowerPoint notes page printout.

Kevin walked wearily into the conference room, nodded to the speechwriter, and plopped into his chair. He addressed Fred: "Thanks for coming. I don't need to rehearse a speech. I think I'm walking into an ambush and I don't believe we've thought carefully enough about what I'm walking into. I wonder whether we can think together for a few hours."

Kevin explained that the next day he would be the sole pharmaceutical executive speaking at a conference of pharmacy benefit managers, the people who negotiate pharmaceutical prices on behalf of insurance companies and others who pay for medicines. He was worried that he would be attacked and wanted to be ready.

Fred began to follow the Q Cycle (Figure 6.1). He began with open-ended, abstract, and complex questions:

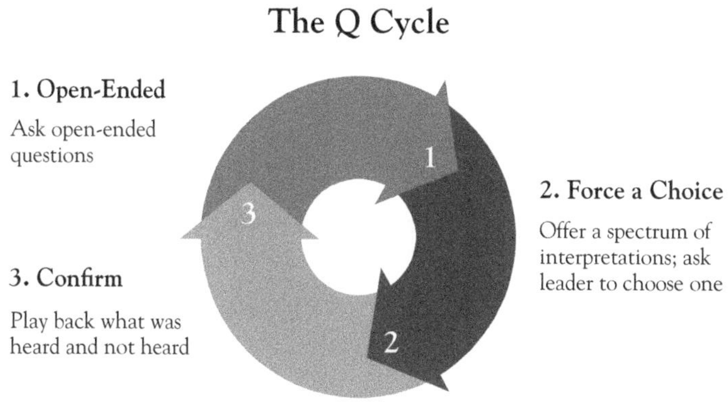

Figure 6.1 The Q Cycle

- Tell me about the conference.
- Help me understand why you said yes to the invitation.
- Why do you think you're the only industry representative there?
- Why do you think you're walking into an ambush?
- What's the big risk you are worrying about?
- Why do you think they invited you?

Fred continued in this vein for about 20 minutes. Then he moved to forcing choices among alternatives.

- Do you think you'll be attacked as an executive of your own company, or as a stand-in for the entire industry?

- Do you think they'll attack a particular medicine your company makes, or the price of medicines in general?
- Do you think they are singling out your company for further pummeling in the future, or is it just that yours is the only company that said Yes to an invitation?

After a while Fred shifted to playing back what he had heard and had not heard:

- So it sounds as if you're there as a proxy for the entire industry. Do you agree?
- I had expected you to wonder why some of your peer companies are not also there, but you haven't raised it. Have you thought about that?
- You began by saying you feared you were walking into an ambush, but I haven't heard you use that kind of alarmist language as you've been describing the conference. Have I missed something?

With that round out of the way, Fred then repeated the cycle on possible approaches Kevin could take; then again with possible messaging he could use.

After a few hours of this, Kevin smiled, stood straight up, shook Fred's hand, and said, "Thanks. I know precisely what I'm going to do and say." The speechwriter perked up and asked, "Should I write it into the speech?" Kevin said, "No, thanks. I know what I'm going to say."

Fred felt sorry for the speechwriter, who had been marginalized. But he was pleased that Kevin had a game plan for how to proceed.

Why Bosses Sometimes Bypass Staff

In that example, Kevin bypassed his speechwriter and instead sought Fred's advice because Kevin didn't think his problem was a bad speech. It was lack of strategic thinking about the risks and opportunities of that particular speaking engagement.

Bosses seek many voices and viewpoints. It's a way to build the evidence necessary for decision-making. But there is also a darker reason. Virtually every top executive we have counseled in our careers can comment instantly on why they feel internal staff or the current group of advisors fall short. These comments should stimulate some serious thinking by those who work internally and seek to be trusted at the top.

"Staff's first inclination is to teach their function," we're often told. Lawyers love the law, finance people love the deal, HR people defend employees, and PR people tend to worry about the news media. Unless you can mention something unique, extraordinarily insightful, or different from these arenas, you are better off focusing on the issues at hand.

We're also told, "Staff people constantly seem to be seeking approval for their behaviors and confirmation of the value they bring, and the value of their function, to everything they do."

It's generally the staff person's tone of voice and choice of words that tend to indicate that somehow the boss is being less than supportive and, in fact, has failed to recognize past contributions. The problem with this discussion, of course, is that almost anything about yesterday has very little interest for the boss. Talk in terms of tomorrow; be known as someone who is facing forward, all the time.

We're told, "Staff people fail to demonstrate that they understand either the business or the key issues the business faces." This problem comes from not knowing the boss better and consequently those issues, problems, and challenges that keep these top people either irritated or energized. You have to talk about both what matters and what's relevant, in the context of the business, circumstance, or issue. It's very wise to apply these same lessons to the needs of senior staff and operational people around the CEO, or senior leaders, as well.

We're told, "They speak a language the boss neither needs nor cares to learn." This is very close to number one where we tend to define everything in terms of our staff function and staff priorities. But mostly it's using words that are neither managerial nor about the future. Yes, you can use words from your functional area or specialty, but they need to be couched and translated into terms managers can work with, understand, and be inspired by.

We're told, "They focus on the unimportant." The most frequent question we find ourselves asking in any discussion is, "Does this really matter?" The topic of discussion may in fact matter, but there needs to be a constant checking and elimination process to stay focused on that magical, powerful 5% that really does matter.

We're told, "They're constantly taking up management's time, telling us things we already know." There's a presumption that management may not necessarily know a lot about what they're getting into, what they're caught up in, or where they're headed, from your perspective. In most of the conversations we are witness to, there is a fair amount of staff educational language that goes on before an advisor actually gets to the point about what they're recommending, suggesting, or illustrating. Our feeling always is, get to the point first and minimize the amount of education required, but the educating is done after the point is made. Give top people credit for knowing things beyond what you know.

We're told, "Press people would rather alienate the boss than a reporter." This is a special caveat for the communications advisor. Almost all executives feel this way; we often refer to this as paycheck confusion. That is, the boss wonders if the communicator actually remembers where the paycheck comes from. "Do they work for me, or for the local newspaper, today?" is something we hear from time-to-time.

The HR advisor is criticized because they are "too soft on people." The lawyer is criticized for stopping something crucial for reasons that are more defensive than strategic.

We're told, "Staff people may write well, but their verbal skills are undisciplined, unfocused, and fail to provide information management can act upon. They have trouble getting to the point." There's something about staff advice that appears based far more on emotion and a kind of staff-driven logic than on facts, data, in-depth knowledge, or experience. This kind of criticism among bosses can be toxic to advisor relationships.

Executives are generally deeply suspicious of intuition—unless it is their own. If you advise a senior executive to do something because you believe in your heart it's the right thing to do, the executive will also look outside to someone else for a more experienced, justifiable, or rational viewpoint.

We're told, "They don't seem to really care, or they seem to have an agenda of their own." In management terms, the issue is loyalty. When you're at the senior levels of an organization or at the very top, you gain a perspective about people and often part of that perspective is a measure of your loyalty and your responsiveness to the individual, again from their perspective. This is at the heart of your relationship and at the heart of trust. It must be dealt with, recognized, and built into the way your relationships with senior executives develop.

You can argue that what you say is far more important than whether or not you are loyal, seem loyal, or can be trusted, simply based on the importance of what you're talking about. However, experience teaches that from a leader's perspective, almost all information they receive comes filtered. The loyal and the trusted can, and are expected to, bring the unvarnished truth.

Whining Turns Bosses Off

The biggest single reason senior executives and CEOs mention to us that they have difficulty working with staff functions in their own organizations is the level to which these functions whine about everything. They whine about budgets, about each other, about the direction things are going, about not being consulted, about the fact that they could have given better information sooner if they had only been included in the discussions. What is fascinating, and a little scary, is that while those are the perceptions of the CEO, staff people have their own whiney excuses for not being in the loop and not being consulted, but if they had been the organization and its leadership would have, could have, should have done better than it did.

Here are the whiniest excuses we hear from staff functions. By the way, bosses know that staff say these things, and it detracts from the staff's credibility and value as members of the team.

- They don't understand the power of my function.
- They don't respect the function.
- They always consult the lawyers and management consultants before they talk to us, and we get stuck cleaning up even bigger messes.
- The CEO's pretty bright but has blind spots and prejudices that get us into trouble.
- We could have told them this was going to happen, but we couldn't break through the silos and the arrogant mentality that, "Management is smart enough to handle anything."
- If I got more face time things would be different.

- Why do they still blame us, but won't talk to us or allow us to have early input?
- Everything is so last minute. Management doesn't follow its own plan (or even have a plan?).

Let us offer some suggestions about other changes you will need to make in your strategy to develop a management perspective: Learn, talk about, and teach things that matter to management. The rest you can practice and use in the privacy of your functional staff activities. To matter to management, you need to provide information and insights that go beyond what the boss or your advisee already knows. After all, if all you do is provide information about stuff they know or have already decided, what value is that? If all you have to offer are the platitudes of your staff function and the simple stuff, it's unlikely you'll be invited back on a regular basis.

Mattering to management also means helping leaders recognize, decide, or identify what to do next. As we discussed previously, as you become more familiar with the world of the CEO, you will discover just how little is planned ahead for decision-making about sources, methods, directions, goals, even aspirations. The ability of an advisor to truly fill in the blank spots or provide sensible alternatives is extraordinarily helpful. Most staff functions, when with the boss, tend to spend more time whining about other staff functions, the value of various service-type activities, and things that have virtually nothing to do with moving the boss's agenda ahead. Come up with an alternative, a new option, a different way of looking at something in the future, and your influence will grow.

Often, identifying the next step seems terribly difficult. You may need to search out, assess, evaluate, and recommend additional sources of expertise of value to those who trust you. Additional brains, experience, data, and insight may be required. Be aggressive and forthright in searching out others with answers or better questions or answers than you. (Among the more difficult choices for the strategic advisor is to be selfless and subservient to the needs of those seeking advice, of being willing to sacrifice or relinquish some personal recognition to assure the relentless, incremental positive progress of those you advise. Doing so can substantially increase your stature and value.)

Be aware of the assumptions that leadership and management use as barriers to advice-givers:

- Managers and leaders inherently feel they are good communicators.
- Operations is always more important than staff functions.
- Some things can never be planned for (like emergencies).
- Things really are better than they seem. We are making progress despite the numbers.
- Outside advice is often more interesting than inside advice.
- Inside advice often seems self-serving.

Understand what you can offer in the way of advice and counsel of a truly strategic nature that may go beyond your staff function, often to a higher level. Ninety-five percent of management decision-making involves operational thinking and execution.

Avoid using dollar equivalent justifications for what you do unless you can clearly and persuasively document a revenue stream into your company or organization, or the actual cost savings as verified by management financial analysis that passes the straight-face test. Management needs proof to believe the dollar value of staff work. Such perceptions have nothing to do with being a Trusted Strategic Advisor, and using a cost-based approach forces management to look at you from a very different perspective. If you set this standard, you will be made to live or die by it.

Focus on outcomes. Focus on tomorrow. Management strategy, management leadership, and management problem-solving are always about tomorrow, even if the topic is yesterday's mistakes.

Make contributions and suggestions that are self-evidently valuable. Here again, if your proposition costs more but adds little extra value, or your suggestion may disrupt the organizational structure without a significant increment of improvement, it's very likely that management will reject what you suggest. Another reason for rejection of advisor ideas is that they tend to promise more than management believes can be delivered. One important secret: make fewer suggestions, but make those you do provide have far greater value than their cost.

The Face Time Fantasy

Virtually every staff advisor we talk with tends to value their actual worth to the boss and senior executives by the amount of face time they get during the day, the week, or the month of the year. Judging by what the boss tells us, this is pure fantasy.

While you are in there talking about grandchildren, fishing, vacations, trips to various places on the planet, the boss—in their mind—is asking these kinds of questions:

- "Why are they wasting my time with this?"
- "How can this possibly matter toward the things I must get done today?"
- "Why don't they have more to do down there that matters?"

What really matters is the value of each minute you have with these people and how you use those minutes. What also matters, of course, is what you recommend that they do. We've mentioned a number of times the importance of being able to make suggestions (rather than new ideas) on the spot, or even multiple suggestions, and how this flies in the face of the executive's ability to get things done. Rather than needing more suggestions, the executive needs fewer more powerful suggestions or options. Rather than spending more time with you face-to-face, the executive needs to spend less time but have that time spent more strategically, more powerfully, and more from a managerial perspective.

Talk to time, write to time. Have a pre-determined strategy, like the three-minute drill, to help ensure that whatever you say, whatever you recommend, you obviously and carefully are making the best use of time. Talking to time overcomes the face-time fantasy. Sensitivity to the time you are taking and the value of the information you are sharing, second-by-second, allows you to have a much more realistic assessment of the value you bring to exchanges you have with senior management. Believe us, they will notice the value as well.

Say Things That Matter

Of all the advice givers in the presence of leadership, the Trusted Strategic Advisor has the absolute obligation to make certain that whatever is offered is truly of value.

Years ago, a former colleague, we'll call her Mary Ann, and Jim were visiting a client involved in very serious litigation. Mary Ann was quite accomplished and has very special expertise on a variety of highly technical areas, one of which was Food and Drug Administration regulation. At the end of a very long, hard day of meetings, client confrontations, and hard work, we were walking to our rental car. Mary Ann asked me, "Did I make much sense today or was I just babbling?"

Jim responded that we always enjoyed her babbling because it was interesting, informed, and often quite entertaining. Then he asked whether she noticed what the really highly respected participants did. They tended to wait until the end of most discussions before beginning to speak. The reason for this, Jim told her quite truthfully, was that whenever they opened their mouths in meetings, whatever was said was expected to be profound, powerful, and essential to everyone. It had to be important. She might consider, Jim suggested, waiting until a bit later in the conversation to begin speaking and make certain that what she said was more functional than conversational. "Say things that matter," he told her.

Mary Ann moved on after five years, and as he does with every employee who leaves, Jim asked her to provide her successor with some tips about how best to work with him—or any boss. Her letter contained a fascinating list of 11 items. In fact, Jim remembered when she learned each of the lessons. There, in number 11, was this lesson. Here is her complete list.

Top 11 Things You Need to Know to Work Successfully with the Boss

1. Prepare work product in final form. It should be your best, most complete effort.
2. Look at situations from a perspective other than the one the boss has—this leads to interesting, productive discussions that ultimately benefit the client with new ideas and approaches.
3. Think, write, and speak in numbers, bullets, and series.

4. Bring your stories, experiences, and personal history to work—often they reflect an approach or strategy you're trying to explain to a client.
5. Recognize, acknowledge, and learn from the mistakes, missteps, gaffes, and goofs you make—then move on.
6. Be solution driven.
7. Be prepared to explain—succinctly and convincingly—your suggestions, proposals, and recommendations. Speak like someone you'd like to listen to.
8. Remain one step ahead and 15 minutes early.
9. Anticipate issues, problems, concerns, and opportunities; prepare the boss before he or the client asks; have a plan.
10. Recognize that not every event is a crisis; respond as if every event is a crisis.
11. Speaking for the sake of speaking is unmemorable—say important things.

Management Perspective Checklist

Here are questions you need to ask yourself about whether you can really put yourself in the boss's shoes and work from a management perspective:

- What is the real expertise you bring to those who run your organization beyond your area of staff knowledge?
- Do you have the patience to make progress incrementally and, at the same time, help the extraordinary number of individuals around you and those who will cross your path as you move toward your goal of becoming a strategic advisor?
- Do you have the stomach for the intensity, conflict, and often-confrontational environment in which decisions are made at the senior levels of organizations?
- Do you have the personal patience and substantive intensity to be able to comfortably hold your own with others who do?

- Can you dispassionately assess the strengths, weaknesses, opportunities, options, and threats of the organization from a variety of useful perspectives?
- Do you have access to those who actually have the operating responsibility to resolve issues, implement solutions, and prevent, detect, or deter unproductive actions?
- What are you providing now that is of real value when the boss makes time to speak with you? What can your boss count on from you if you are called in ahead of everyone else?

7 Think Strategically

Chapter Outline

The concepts and ideas behind being strategic, including the nine virtues of a strategist, the four phases of strategic thinking, and the five barriers that hold strategists back. Find out how much of a strategist you are.

Every staff function seems concerned about being more strategic.

The word strategy and the word strategic are among the most overused by staff people and management. Despite overuse, there still appears to be little evidence that staff people truly understand what it means to be strategic or to be able to recognize what a strategy is. Since our backgrounds are in communication, we got tired of hearing these words quite early in our careers, only to find that these words were used in every other staff function, too. In human resources, the legal department, security, finance, IT, even Facilities Management, "being a strategic player" and similar notions saturate the staff environment.

Jim was once asked to speak at the inaugural meeting of a special trade association consisting solely of the chief litigation officers for America's largest companies. He was clearly somewhat puzzled when he got the request to speak. The gentlemen who contacted Jim said, "We'd like to hear your presentation on developing a strategic mindset." Jim's response was, "I'm not an attorney. I work with lots of attorneys, but attorneys seem to have a fair amount of juice on their own. Your members must represent literally hundreds of trillions of dollars of potential sales and revenue to your client organization." He agreed. So, Jim asked, "They have problems getting to the table anyway?"

The response astounded Jim. "Even having these very significant dollar responsibilities, attorneys feel that they have difficulty with and little status in the operational decision-making process. Attorneys feel that clients don't listen to or simply ignore their advice." Here comes the shocker: "We need to be at the table much more frequently, preferably, all the time." Jim had thought that attorneys were always successful in getting themselves welded to the hips of most senior executives.

Well, imagine that: attorneys feeling that they are not at the table, either. The rest of us tend to feel that only the attorneys get heard. At the conference, after Jim's talk, the questions from these high-powered corporate lawyers were simple, direct, yet often as naïve as he hears from any other staff function. Fred also has had similar requests, from organizations of defense counsel. They don't have a problem getting to the table during litigation. But they're not asked to the table as business advisors. And it's precisely as business advisors that they can provide input that could potentially prevent litigation into the future.

The Strategic Perspective

This "lack of hearing" by those in operations causes a tension between staff functions and operating activities that can get in the way of building relationships. Prepare to move beyond this tension by focusing on how to move issues and questions forward from an operating perspective.

Developing a strategic mindset is crucial to having the relationship, influence, and access that most staff people crave, or feel entitled to. We begin the process of thinking about developing a strategic mindset by understanding what strategy is. Jim has a rather unusual approach. You have achieved a strategic mindset when you are able to verbally inject mental energy into an organization's operational processes to help leaders and their organization achieve management objectives.

Fred has a similar idea, expressed a bit differently. Fred describes strategy as the alignment of any given task to the fulfillment of a clearly defined purpose. A strategic mindset, what Fred describes as being habitually strategic, is the capacity to defer decisions on tactics—what to do—until there's clarity of why to do it. To fulfill a purpose. Or as Jim puts it, to achieve management objectives.

Strategy is the most crucial product of leadership. It is the ability to be strategic that defines the value of a leader. The reality, as we have seen, is that the higher one goes in an organization, the less actual hands-on the work leaders have or need to do. The leader's attention becomes divided among teaching and leading people in the right direction; observing, correcting, and tweaking what is actually going on; and, much of the time, looking over the horizon to identify future destinations and the directions to get to the future, and the people necessary to make it happen.

Becoming a strategist means committing to a mental approach that outthinks the competition, the opposition, or the critics and produces a distinctive or unique approach, series of steps, solution options, or direction choices.

Strategic energy is what drives businesses and organizations, guides leaders, and sets the directions for teams, players, employees, customers, and others. Strategy is the attractant that draws people together and helps them focus on moving in the same direction. Strategy is among the most positive and energizing states of mind. Most of us gravitate toward strategists and leaders for this very reason: they know where we're going, and they have some idea of what our destination is, even if they have very little information on the specifics or the mechanics of actually getting there.

Strategy focuses the energy and momentum for whatever the current plan of action happens to be. Assuming that the current plan is based on fundamentally sound information, the advisor's question is, "What part of the overall strategy is your part of the plan accomplishing, enhancing, or advancing?"

Strategy Is Always Positive

Strategy is always positive and future focused. To strategize about the past is a contradiction. Looking backward is usually negative and is done only within strict, useful guidelines such as pattern recognition, as described in Chapter 8. The strategic thinker is a positive force. This positive focus is what we expect or at least hope for from leaders.

Behaviors that keep us focused on the past are clearly non-strategic, for example, debating the past, focusing on the unimportant, labeling actions and ideas as strategic (whether they actually are or not), being negative ("can't do that," "I don't like it," and so on), and making excuses. Teaching the value of staff functions and similar behaviors rather than showing new strategic insights drains influence and organizational energy and blocks forward momentum. The wise advisor carefully avoids sounding like a schoolmarm.

The Eight Virtues of a Strategist

The place to begin assessing your strategic capacity is by asking yourself critical questions about how you approach ideas, questions, opportunities, dangers, and challenges. Use these questions as tools to develop your personal behaviors. You might refer to them as "The Virtues of the Strategist." Virtues are principles and guidelines for your thinking, behavior, and recommendations. Sometimes they are expressions of your intentions.

This is an exercise you can do privately to determine just how strategic you really are or can be. Try it. Assess yourself against these seven strategic thinking guidelines or virtues.

1. **Inconsistency**

   The strategist is intentionally inconsistent. In strategy, inconsistency is a virtue. Strategists relentlessly question all assumptions. The goal, always, is to identify a different approach, to discover new options to try new and unconventional combinations of ideas and concepts. Remember most of man's greatest discoveries were accidents, mistakes, and miscalculations.

   Are you predictable? Do you approach most problems in the very same way? Is what you recommend and think about virtually the same every time? Are you bound up every time, looking at everything through the lens of your staff function?

   Be intentionally different. Grab the wrong end of the telescope. Think about things from a different perspective, intentionally, relentlessly.

   Advisors of the highest value to leaders and managers are often those who can see things from an entirely different perspective.

When you study military strategists, for example, Sun Tzu, von Clausewitz, B. H. Liddell Hart, and others, notice that each of them stresses that the key to victory is acting differently than the opponent expects.

A client of Jim's who operated an educational facility for special children was in a situation where a teacher mistakenly loaned a student a videotape of sexually explicit material that was shown to the student's family. The child's father was so irate he rushed to the school, beat up the teacher, hired a lawyer, and threatened to sue, all in the first three hours of the incident. Standard procedure for responding to allegations is to sit tight, let a little time pass, and see if cooler heads can prevail or a simple solution might emerge.

Jim's approach was to move much more aggressively. The allegations from this incident were potentially explosive. Having worked through similar situations in the past, one big lesson he learned is that bad situations like this one ripen badly. In highly emotional situations such as this one, unless dealt with positively and promptly, anger, irritation, suspicion, and emotion tend to grow quickly and to cloud the issues, to confuse the victims, even to confuse those whose job is to fix the situation.

Since the head of the school was a man about the same age as the father, and they both had boys the same age, Jim suggested that the president immediately write a letter of sympathy, explanation, and apology to this father and offer to meet promptly to work out whatever problems might have been caused by the event. After a brief conversation with the client's attorneys, it was agreed that the letter should be sent directly to the victim's father.

As expected, the father's attorney called, boiling mad, and demanded to know whose idea it was to send this letter. He threatened to file an ethics violation with the local bar association against legal counsel. However, Jim knew that because the president of the company was not a lawyer, the father of the boy was not an attorney, and Jim was not an attorney, they were not subject to the rules of legal procedure. Had they followed legal procedure, it might have taken days, weeks, or longer even to get a meeting to talk about the situation. As it turned out, this very prompt action, the day of the event, triggered a series of meetings that began within 72 hours, and a settlement occurred within five working days. The speed and effectiveness of this rapid approach is now standard operating procedures for this organization. The cost savings in legal fees is enormous, while the settlements achieved are fast, fair, and generally, those affected, remain clients and customers.

Avoid creating a black hole from which you cannot escape. Stalling, delaying, avoiding positive action when there are victims, whatever the reason, you get sucked into a black hole you can never credibly or believably explain.

2. Real Expertise

Technically, your staff function defines the expertise you bring to the table. Being strategic means using your staff experience as a platform to learn even more about the operating areas of the business. You do this for two reasons. First, most operating executives believe they are sufficiently competent in staff areas and their need for advice about staff activities is minimal. Second, delving successfully and deeply into an operating area builds your value to management and provides more common ground on which to converse, advise, and assist with operating executives.

A colleague of Jim's was once approached by a very large refuse hauling company to bid on some work. As he assessed the prospect of doing this, he was warned that this particular company was founded by garbage men and tended to hire only other garbage men. So, Jim's colleague went to his local trash hauler, and in exchange for signing a rather complicated and comprehensive release, was allowed to ride on a garbage truck for five days to see what these people do every single day. The garbage truck is the cash register of the business. Garbage companies make money every time a big bucket of trash is dumped into the back of a truck.

As he tells the story, the moment he sat down with his prospective client, he began talking about his experience. He struck a chord with those in the room, and ultimately wound up becoming a long-term, outside advisor to this organization. You could argue that riding on a truck for a few days really isn't substantive expertise, but you also have to admit that very few of us have ever ridden on a garbage truck for even a few minutes, much less five days. It was a pretty impressive approach to understanding what the business is really all about from where the manager or boss comes from.

3. **Substantive Intensity**

A strategist applies focus and intensity to the most critical parts of a problem or opportunity using fact-finding, truth-seeking, and reality testing. The goal is to help everyone focus on the 5% that really matters.

Do you focus primarily on a single aspect of an issue? Do you see problems, issues, and priorities from the boss's perspective? Can you adequately assess and execute the operating benefits of your responsibility? Can you hold your own when the conversation turns to operational concerns?

Jim rarely attends strategic planning meetings. In fact, Jim rarely attends meetings he is not leading or playing a significant role in. However, on one occasion, he was asked by the CEO to sit in and help work through the process of establishing a 5- to 10-year, forward-looking picture for the company. They had hired a very experienced facilitator from one of the large consulting companies. He had an excellent reputation.

As the meeting opened, it was clear that there was going to be some difficulty in establishing a timeframe in which to hypothesize. After 45 minutes of struggle to get some traction, Jim raised his hand and asked the CEO how long he had been in office. He replied, "About 20 months." Jim then asked how long his predecessor had served as CEO. He said, "About 37 months." Jim then asked about the predecessor before that and his answer was, "About 42 months." Jim then turned and suggested to the facilitator and the group, "Why don't we begin by hypothesizing the next 18 to 20 months, the likely length of time the current CEO will be in office, and see where that will take us." There was a noticeable gasp in the group, followed by a short period of silence. Jim was sure that they were all thinking that his service as a consultant had just ended. However, the meeting got on track almost immediately and they were able to move forward to a more satisfactory set of ideas and concepts. Jim did get to go home early. He was invited back the next day to continue a more focused approach.

The question you're asking constantly to achieve and maintain substantive intensity is, "Does what we're doing now really matter?" If not, move on, or end the meeting.

4. **Laggership**

This concept means acting promptly, rather than immediately. It's waiting, or standing back, just momentarily.

The analogy for Laggership is the military patrol, exploring enemy territory. The shortest life expectancy is for the person at the point of the patrol who will have first contact. Our preference is to be in the third or fourth ranks so that we have the opportunity to see where the bullets are coming from and have a better chance to survive to return and report to headquarters.

Taking a moment to get grounded, to understand the situation you face, can be liberating. Fred often quotes Stephen Covey, author of *The 7 Habits of Highly Effective People*, who wrote a forward to a book on the principles of the noted Austrian psychiatrist Viktor E. Frankl, the founder of the logotherapy school of psychiatry, which focuses on the search for meaning. In that foreword, Covey describes a central element of Frankl's philosophy: "Between stimulus and response, there is a space. In that space lies our freedom and our power to choose our response." This aptly describes the power strategic advisors have to move their clients to success Covey argues that the brief pause helps us harness the power to choose our response to our circumstances.

5. **Entropy**

This is a term from physics that describes and predicts that virtually all systems and activities will degrade, decline, and disintegrate without the addition or injection of energy and resources. Fail to service your car regularly and it will become unsafe and eventually fall apart. Fail to nurture and maintain relationships, and they too degrade and eventually come apart.

These two concepts are related and are quite strategic in their application to management decision-making. Most staff people have a bias for action. The strategist looks at a range of action options. The choice of action options comes only after study and evaluation within the context of these seven virtues.

6. **Pragmatism**

A strategist attempts to clarify, refine, and carefully target; to deal in facts, truth, and reality-based information; and, wherever possible, to forecast results that can actually or reasonably be achieved while recognizing the consequences of various action options. A pragmatist usually forecasts underwhelming results.

Another way Jim defines a pragmatist is an individual who can see the doable, know the knowable, get the getable, and achieve the achievable.

Pragmatism is often considered the opposite, or certainly very different from optimism. Over-optimism and the failure to accurately estimate, evaluate, and forecast the outcomes of their activities are the two most significant reasons leaders lose their positions.

Pragmatism is the antidote for excessive optimism. Can you and do you accurately forecast the intended and unintended results of your recommendations?

7. **Focus**

This is a Peter F. Drucker concept. It's what gets done that matters. The strategist focuses on what the business needs to get done, in priority order. The strategist consistently asks, "What is the singular importance of what I'm doing? What is its relevance to achieving management's most crucial objectives?"

Constantly gravitating toward the most important actions, decisions, behaviors, and outcomes is a key ingredient in being an effective strategist.

8. **Incrementalism**

Anyone who has run anything for any length of time learns pretty quickly that all progress occurs in increments and rarely in giant leaps. Proposals and ideas that suggest that giant leaps are possible are generally suspect in operational terms.

The strategist recognizes that most everything in the life of an organization gets done one step at a time and sometimes in only fractions of a step at a time. The issue is absolute progress rather than the quantity or even the quality of the progress. It is the relentless desire and urgency to move ahead, to find the next constructive increment, and achieve it, so we can see what the next progress increment could be.

Do you manage the expectations of those you advise? Can you candidly explore the limitations of your own thinking and ideas?

Thinking Strategically

Many years ago, Jim came across an interesting concept by the Japanese consultant Kenichi Ohmae. His book *The Mind of the Strategist: Business Planning for Competitive Advantage* provided an epiphany for Jim on page 14 of the paperback edition, through an illustration he called, "The Mind of a Strategist."[1]

Ohmae's key insight is his analysis comparing three management-thinking methodologies: mechanical systems thinking (Jim calls this "linear thinking"), intuition, and strategic thinking.

Let's talk about each of them as we've come to understand them and teach them to others.

Linear Thinkers

The linear thinker or process thinker, if you prefer, is the trained or experienced manager, boss, or specialist; the physician, the economist, the MBA, the engineer, the scientist, or your typical CEO. This thinking is typified by a more structured, process-driven, or linear approach. Linear thinkers are the people who, as Dr. Stephen Covey would say, plan with the end in mind, using management structure and formats, chronologies, order of manufacture, etc. It is how the doctor, lawyer, engineer, MBA, operations manager, or boss gets things done.

Virtually all senior leaders are largely linear thinkers. Figure 7.1 illustrates the heart of the management thinking process. When confronted with a problem, the manager's first step is to divide that problem into its major constituent elements (see the roman numerals one through five) and then to begin working and re-working those elements over time (see the arrow on the right) for the purpose of arriving at a solution, answer, idea, or forecast. When planning, the end to be achieved or the problem to be resolved is identified early (maybe years earlier), and a process is constructed backwards to include every detail, up to and through start-up or start-over to achieve

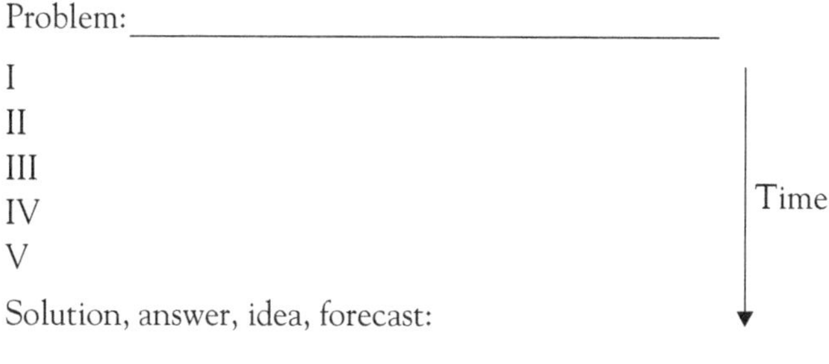

Figure 7.1 Management Thinking (Linear, Process)

the goal. It is a process approach, predictable but useful for its simplicity, structure, and focus on resolution.

Linear thinkers are the people who can easily intimidate creative or intuitive people because linear thinkers seem so organized, so "logical," so . . . well, linear. It is a serious discipline to become and remain a linear thinker—to constructively see the world in process increments. It's part of developing a management mindset (see Chapter 3). Actually, management may relate better to the staff functions that use similar thinking and intellectual strategies—law, finance, accounting, and IT—than with the more intuitive approaches of communications, human resources, or strategic planning.

Intuitive Thinkers

The contrast to linear thinking is highly intuitive thinking, which is used especially in communications, human resources, and to some extent in security.

The intuitive thinker is a person whose brain has a significant amount of stuff "floating around" that "gets triggered" by having to find immediate or deadline-driven solutions and answers. The process and intuitive styles are vastly different and often conflicted ways of thinking. People who are creators such as artists, painters, news reporters, inventors, and writers are intuitive thinkers. Corporate functions requiring high levels of creativity or people-focus also tend to be highly intuitive, that is to say, human resources, communications, security, and strategic planning.

Intuitive people often actually avoid analytical approaches. The goal is to find the great idea and/or the most interesting or creative solution—the silver bullet, or a non-linear solution because the issues faced are highly emotional or perceptual. Linear thinkers are often frustrated by the extemporaneous nature of intuitive advice.

If you're an intuitive thinker, chances are you can operate on pretty short deadlines, marshal a lot of information relatively quickly, and be ready to act on short notice. Also, ideas come far more rapidly to the intuitive thinker than to the linear or process thinker. In fact, painters, writers, creative types are mainly intuitive thinkers and their brains, in a sense, are like huge storage houses (Jim often makes the comparison to wastebaskets as a better concept) for dozens, perhaps thousands of ideas and fragments of thoughts. Any number of these fragments can be activated and articulated through an experience, a word, a photograph, or someone else's presentation.

In Figure 7.2, each dot or circle represents an experience, some fragment or factoid, idea or concept, simply floating around in the intuitive thinker's mind waiting to be activated, primarily by a deadline rather than a process.

While the linear thinker is driven by a timeline, a chronology, and a structured outline with basically all of its elements known, the intuitive thinker is simply driven by the deadline—ingredients floating around suddenly come together to produce the desired effect or outcome. There is little long-range thinking about how things will turn out. With the intuitive thinker, it is all very last minute. With the intuitive thinker, if there is no deadline, there is no progress, or solution.

It is this spontaneous, seeming shallowness and lack of evidence that makes the linear thinker uncomfortable about intuition-driven approaches.

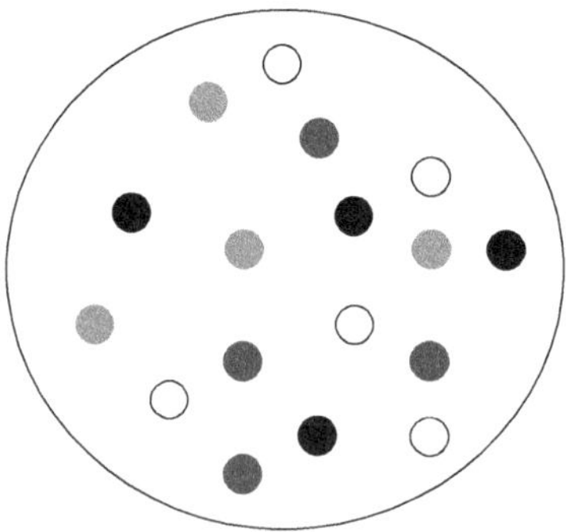

Figure 7.2 Intuitive Thinking

This frustrates the intuitive thinker because, "they (linear thinkers) just don't get it."

For advice to be recognized, understood, and taken seriously, intuitive thinking must be translated into a process methodology. Translating thinking strategies into process makes them easier for managers to absorb and act upon. Intuitive thinkers translate their ideas and concepts into the process methodology in three ways, through the creation of checklists, prioritized lists, or sequences of events. The Three-Minute Drill in Chapter 9 is an extremely useful translation tool in this regard.

Strategic Thinkers

The strategic thinker intentionally takes an entirely different approach—every time. All assumptions are suspended. Inconsistency is a key goal of strategic thinking. The strategist consciously, relentlessly, and purposely seeks different approaches. The strategist is intentionally going for an unusual, unexpected result.

Paraphrasing Ohmae's interpretation, strategic thinking is a process involving four phases: problem identification; analysis and weighing of constituents; deconstruction, scenario development based on different constituent configurations or options; and creative re-integration. The goal is to intentionally achieve or select an unusual result.

One of Jim's favorite stories about strategic thinking comes from Dr. Edward DeBono.[2] As he describes the situation in Great Britain early in World War II when the Battle of Britain was going on and the Germans were inflicting enormous losses on British aircraft, British engineers were working constantly to reinforce the airplanes against damage from attack but their efforts were largely unsuccessful. It was a frustrating and frightening time.

Then, after weeks of constantly studying the aircraft returning to Britain that had survived the enemy, one engineering group had an unusual idea. Rather than reinforcing the damaged areas on the returning aircraft they could see, why not reinforce the areas that were not damaged, which the engineers couldn't see because the destroyed aircraft were never recovered for analysis. This dramatic change in thinking had a significant impact on the survivability of aircraft and was one of the ingredients that helped Britain prevail in the air battles leading up to the major actions in World War II.

Applying Thinking Styles to Problem-Solving

Examination of Mr. Ohmae's diagram shows just how different the three thinking styles are. The same problem is examined in the context of each thinking style.

Phase One: Problem Identification

- The linear thinker begins applying a symmetrical concepts approach, more to reconfigure than to re-invent.
- The intuitive thinker immediately begins to seek a critical fact, idea, notion, or insight among a host of other potential ideas and concepts.
- The strategic thinker is, literally, from the start, creatively deconstructing the problem in ways that are unique and outside of expected patterns. The pattern of assumptions made by the intuitive and linear thinkers is totally challengeable in the strategist's mind.

Phase Two: Differentiation

- The linear thinker begins in a symmetrical way looking to reconfigure the problem in various, sometimes even innovative ways.
- The intuitive thinker seeks to begin pushing away the extraneous, continuing to seek a significant idea or approach.
- The strategic thinker continues purposely deconstructing the problem in ways that are different, unusual, and searching for a surprising result.

Phase Three: Deconstruction

- All three thinking styles are beginning to fashion their solutions and are at the extreme edge of their approach to deconstructing the problem.

Phase Four: Creative Re-integration

- During this phase, the linear thinker has produced a fairly symmetrical concept that may actually be quite innovative but is also expected or predictable.
- The intuitive thinker has found the silver bullet, the big idea, and will take it to management as the magic solution for a problem.
- The strategic thinker has developed a decidedly non-linear complex, unexpected, even strange response. This is what strategic thinkers do.

> They are inconsistent; they are different; they think from different altitudes and attitudes with the goal of coming up with something unique, hopefully important, powerful, and conclusive.

As you compare these approaches in Mr. Ohmae's diagram, Figure 7.3 is a graphic illustration of the differences in the product these thinking styles produce.

The linear thinker's result is symmetrical. It adds up, has balance, and to a certain degree resembles the original problem.

This comment can be confusing. The example Jim often uses involves big organizations coming out of bankruptcy or other powerful business situations, where the changes they ultimately make after much study, investment, and the gnashing of teeth, seem relatively minor. An airline comes out of bankruptcy, and the first thing it does is to repaint the aircraft and change the company stationary. You could characterize this solution as resembling the original problem or a large retailer, following a huge reorganization, taking as its first initiative, changing the uniforms of those who work with customers.

The intuitive solution is the classic "silver bullet." This is the response, idea, or action that will solve the problem in one amazing, perhaps single, action or activity. These are extraordinarily rare. Few examples really come to mind: Penicillin, an accidental discovery; the transistor, the result of a brainstorm of scientists at Bell Laboratories; the light bulb, a simple device invented by Thomas Edison after 5,000 unsuccessful attempts; the I-beam architecture used in buildings that led to structures so high that elevators were invented to replace staircases; the World Wide Web. While dramatic and interesting, these life and society-changing concepts are very, very few indeed.

The strategist's solution often looks very little like the original problem. And, in fact, utilizing elements of the original problem produces a distinct and unique solution. A strategist's goal is to transform the problem prototype into a command opportunity, a command strategy, a series of actions leading to a powerful result, or series of results. Clearly, strategic thinking is the most challenging of the three. The goals are different and its approaches are different. In many respects, the product of strategic thinking can make management action very unconventional but also very powerful.

In real life, good managers and decision-makers, even staff people, are situational thinkers. They can be process sensitive. They can be intuitive. They

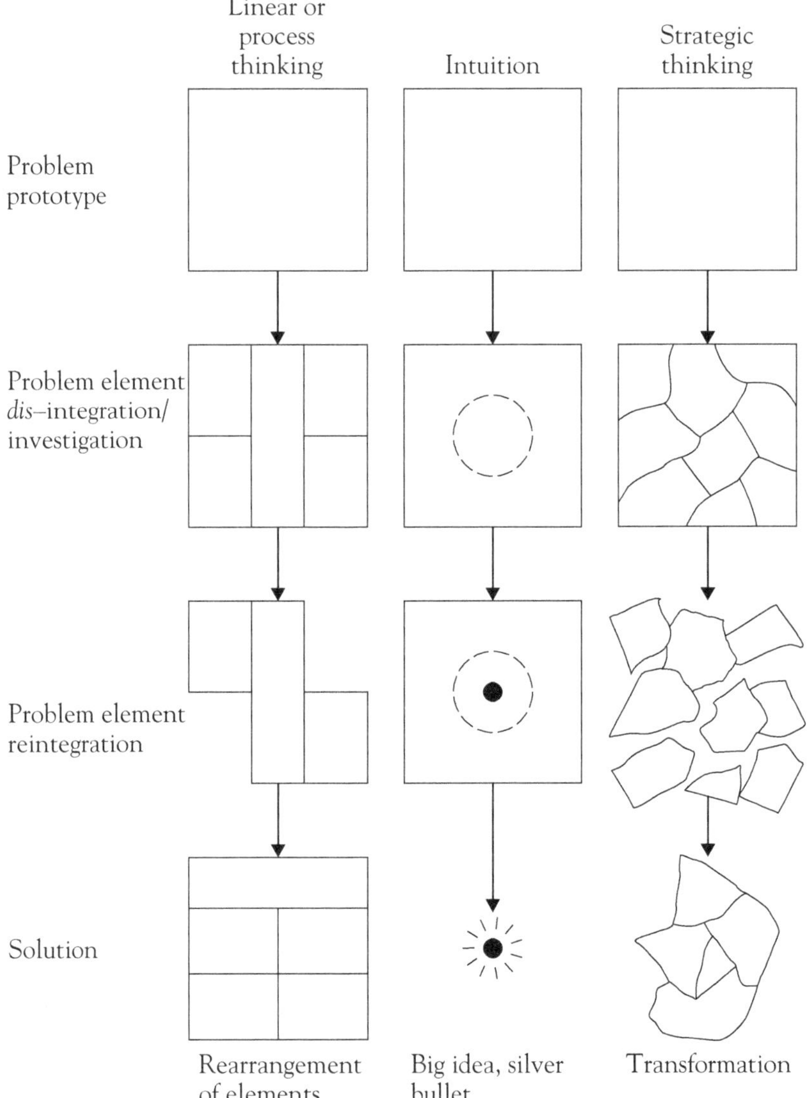

Figure 7.3 The Mindset of a Strategist

can be strategic. For an organization to execute a strategy there must be a process for integrating and implementing strategy translated into language and action plans that those affected can understand, support, and execute.

Why Some Strategies Never Get Off the Ground Many proposed strategies—seemingly brilliant though they may be in the eyes of staff advisors—never make if off the drawing board, never get implemented. Some strategies can't be executed for lots of pretty simple reasons—they're unworkable, unethical, sometimes irresponsible, or they may be unpowerful. In our experience, there are five most common ingredients of strategic failure. These are examples of fatal flaws in strategy:

1. **Not really part of a strategic interest.** A strategy may be foolproof, but if its objective doesn't align with the larger corporate strategy, it is beside the point.
2. **Management can't support.** Some solutions or strategies may be too complicated—may cut across too many internal political and operational barriers, create substantial unintended future consequences, or simply seem too risky.
3. **Developed without input from the boss.** This is probably the most common reason for strategies to fail. Staff people mistakenly work through elaborate processes and procedures, getting everything "ready-to-go" and then present their findings or approaches to the boss who is, of course, totally stunned by what has gone on, especially since there was no input from the boss in the first place.
4. **Usurps the legitimate territory of others.** This might be better stated, "Gives the appearance of infringing on the territory of others as recognized by the others." Aside from death by question, the complaint that some course of action originated in the wrong place within the organization is quite often difficult to overcome or can even be insurmountable.
5. **Avoids dealing with truly tough stuff.** Where are those advisors who told the hundreds of American CEOs that backdating stock options was, "probably legal"? They are gone, but so are the CEOs, general counsels, and CFOs. When staff keep quiet to protect their jobs rather than ruffle feathers by offering the strategies,

options, and warnings bosses need to survive truly critical situations, career defining moments often occur.

Becoming and being a strategic player is a difficult and challenging discipline to master. Most management environments treat those who are inconsistent and challenging as argumentative and obstructive. At first, you'll learn to put your strategic hat on only when those things that really matter are at stake. Having some success with this approach will embolden you to adopt more broadly strategic behaviors and attitudes. Management will need to test before they trust, verify before they trust, authenticate before they trust. Keep the positive pressure on and the value of your strategic efforts will powerfully speak for itself.

Can You Develop a Strategic Mindset?

As I noted at the outset of the chapter, staff people love to use the language of strategy. But many do not get beyond the words "strategy" and "strategic" to actually thinking and acting strategically. Here are some questions to ask yourself:

1. Can you develop a flexible approach to problems? (Or do you approach most problems in the very same way every time?)
2. Have you developed an understanding of the business that goes beyond your staff function?
3. Can you see problems, issues, and priorities from the boss's perspective?
4. Do you understand how your actions and advice are relevant to achieving management's most crucial objectives?
5. Are you constantly asking yourself, does this really matter?
6. Do you have a bias for action—but only after you have studied the lay of the land?
7. Do you focus on what is doable rather than the ideal?
8. Can you candidly explore the limitations of your own thinking and ideas?

If you can give a positive answer to most of these questions, you are well on the way to developing a strategic mindset.

8 The Power of Patterns

Chapter Outline

One of the great insights into being a powerful forecaster is understanding how to learn the patterns of past experiences. Learn the five lessons for working with patterns and recognizing threats.

Some time ago, the chairman and chief executive of a large regional bank, headquartered in the southeastern United States, invited Jim to work with his chief operating officer to improve the COO's board presentation skills and prepare him for some extensive public visibility with respect to a new regional corporate initiative. Little did Jim anticipate the fireworks that began shortly after he arrived.

Their initial meeting was scheduled to take place in the corporate training center, which had the appropriate technology and support facilities. Jim arrived early; the COO, who was almost always early, wasn't there. At the appointed time for the meeting to begin, Jim called the COO's office to check with his secretary. She told Jim that as far as she knew he had planned to be there, it was on the calendar, they had talked earlier that morning, and the meeting was the plan. After an hour, there was still no chief operating officer.

Ninety minutes into their scheduled meeting time, the COO arrived, obviously upset, irritated, and about to explode. His first comment was, "I'm going to kill the S.O.B." Jim's response was, "And which S.O.B. would that be?" His response was, "There's only one," and he named, of course, the chairman. Clearly, the agenda for the day had just evaporated so Jim asked him to grab a cup of coffee, sit down, and they would talk it through. As it turns out, the COO had breakfast that morning with the chairman who casually informed him that he was contemplating putting the bank up for sale. This infuriated the COO, of course, because up until breakfast time, he'd assumed, with positive indications from the chairman, that he was going to be the new chief executive upon the boss's retirement. All that was about to change; 20 years of work, dedication, and anticipation were about to be flushed down the drain.

Incidentally, during Jim's briefing by the chairman about what he expected from the work Jim was to do with the chief operating officer, the chairman told Jim that he was planning to retire within 24 months and that unless something happened during that time frame the chief operating officer would be his successor. That was extremely confidential. Jim kept that to himself.

The COO and Jim spent the next two hours walking through the inevitable and incredible pattern that virtually all succession strategies experience: the first being, of course, to review the three main stages of leadership of an organization; finding the bathroom, getting something done, and establishing one's legacy or immortality. Clearly, the chairman was moving seriously into the immortality phase.

There's nothing like a succession scenario to trigger the yearning in the chief executive to be remembered permanently in the future and to make every effort to ensure that their pet projects, ideas, and concepts cannot be changed by some future CEO, even if that individual is of their own choosing. Every time CEOs leave an organization, their thoughts turn to legacy and immortality.

Jim and the COO talked about likely scenarios, the first, of course, being that the longer the chairman stays in office, contemplating succession, the less likely it is that his first choice, this COO, will survive the gauntlet the chairman will create during the next 24 months. There's a definite behavior shift where CEOs begin to torpedo their putative successors. In fact, anytime a retirement is announced more than 10 or 12 months into the future, the likely successor at the time of the announcement is less and less likely to be the successor when retirement ultimately occurs. What gets executed is the successor's career. Count on this as part of the pattern.

The COO and Jim talked about many things that day, but the most important were these: becoming the successor was up to the successor to accomplish, rather than the CEO. "Starting today, suck it up, deal with it, keep your temper in check, and focus on getting through what's about to happen," Jim said. Jim told the COO to expect the CEO to invent lots of new ideas, micromanage, and intervene. The closer retirement gets the more many CEOs feel the place still needs them to survive. Since, in this case, the CEO had decided he wanted to try to sell the bank, the COO's job, first and foremost, as the COO, was to step forward and volunteer to chair the selling effort, and to carry it out with the highest level of effectiveness.

Jim and the COO also talked about the fact that whatever the chairman has done can be undone the moment the successor takes office. "Stop worrying about what's not getting done," Jim told him. "Many of the things you'd like to do to prepare for succession will be blocked, and you will be prohibited from doing anything substantive until you have those magic three letters,

CEO, by your name. It's true, selling the company can change all of that, but the odds of selling this bank, at this time, in this market, involved a great deal of optimism."

"But he's not making any efforts or steps to plan for a transition period," the COO complained. My response was, "Well, duh. If he gets hit by a bus tomorrow, you can step in. If you can survive for 24 months, he'll allow you to succeed him and you can step in then. Transition and succession is often something only management theorists from business schools tend to idealize and write about."

After they met for about five and a half hours, the COO went back to his office to organize his thoughts with a whole new perspective on how to survive the next 24 months. Jim walked over to see the chairman and tell him three things:

1. This was the last assignment that he could do for him since he had selected new leadership and Jim's attention now had to shift to the COO's best interests.
2. That the CEO should grab his wife of 37 years, rent a Winnebago next week, take a corporate checkbook along, and visit every one of their 340 branches throughout the Southeast, write checks, get in the newspaper, have community dinners and celebrations of this institution's work in the community and his personal work, and this vision of his impending retirement. This would allow the COO to learn to run the place in his absence.
3. Surprise everyone by retiring at least nine to 10 months ahead of his announced schedule.

With that, Jim left and went back to New York. Essentially, that was that. Actually, that was the only time Jim spent with the chief operating officer and the last time he spent any time with the CEO.

Seven years, almost to the day, after that meeting, Jim got a phone call from the COO, who introduced himself as the CEO of the bank. He asked whether Jim remembered him, and Jim said that he certainly did. The CEO said that he was beginning to contemplate his own retirement, and he recalled that he and Jim had met for a single day that had transformed his circumstances at the time. He didn't remember precisely what happened during that day, but he wondered if Jim was still helping in succession situations. Would Jim mind if his intended successor called him to get some advice.

Jim responded that he remembered the day minute-by-minute and if he'd like to review it, he'd be happy to refresh his memory. Perhaps he'd like to have Jim do it with his successor on the line. Or, of course, his successor could give him a call. And, by the way, Jim asked him what his intended retirement date was. He laughed and said, "Well, it's coming up pretty quickly, about six to eight months."

His successor never did call, but Jim knows for a fact that the transition went off without a hitch. Last he heard, the just retired CEO was riding around the southeastern United States in a large bus, with a company checkbook, writing checks, and celebrating the new era in his company and its new leadership.

Study the Patterns of Past Scenarios

Both Jim and Fred, independently of each other and then together, discovered the power of patterns early in their careers. In Fred's academic work he studies patterns of leadership, of language, of stakeholder reaction to language. He studies patterns of crises and patterns of social change.

Patterns have two kinds of power: explanatory power, helping make sense of things that happened before; and predictive power, helping foresee what is likely to happen in the future. Looking back, we can discern what never works, and looking forward, we can seek to avoid what we conclude never works. Similarly, looking back we can discern what always works, and looking forward we can seek to do what always works.

Some say that history repeats itself, and that those who fail to study and learn from history are doomed to repeat it. Our experience is the opposite. No matter how much we study history, we will undoubtedly repeat significant portions of it. But we can be selective in just what we repeat. The objective of pattern analysis is to pay strategic attention to what the key elements, timelines, and repetitive events reveal, and use those insights to forecast the future.

It's the repetitive patterns of decisions, behaviors, and mistakes that key historical events illustrate, often in the same order, that are the incentives to study them as potential future scenarios. Such awareness provides significant insight into likely event sequences, actions, or decision schedules, and to explore the range of outcomes and the options available to change outcomes.

Often when we talk about this, especially in connection with the scenario planning required to be appropriately prepared for many serious management situations, the pushback we both get is that a particular client's market, culture, product line, or history is so unique that what's happened before can't possibly be relevant to what's going to happen. But that is wishful thinking on the client's part.

Experience teaches the opposite. But we still hear the old bromide that a "cookie cutter" approach will fail. What you learn as a strategic advisor is that quite often a cookie cutter will help stabilize the situation and begin to counteract the new patterns so there is far less damage from collateral consequences caused by genuinely new or unique aspects of the new situation. The reality of what patterns teach is that cookie cutters actually work, again, and again, and again, precisely because history does repeat itself. Cookie cutters actually allow for faster response to urgent situations and provide immediate, experientially based action options. It beats guessing and the communal decision-making so evident when management is faced with unfamiliar, explosive, or toxic circumstances.

In the last chapter, we talked about inconsistency as a virtue of strategy. Now that you are studying the value of patterns, it seems that there is a contradiction here. But, in fact, one of the brain-busting attributes of strategists is that they can deal with this kind of ambiguity and resist the urge to set absolute pathways for making important decisions. The strategist relies on a variety of tools and disciplines, and among the most important is a healthy skepticism about the past. Patterns are helpful because they lead to the future, but they are also risky because they allow us to make assumptions based on the past that may or may not be helpful or even true. Rather than be confused, accept the fact that pattern expertise is an essential discipline. Each of us needs to look carefully at all patterns for our own inherent inconsistencies.

The Strategic Value of Pattern-Related Thinking

If you understand patterns, if you systematically discipline yourself to observe events and scenarios with an eye for analyzing event structure, timelines, and variables, two powerful benefits accrue to you: first, you simply know more than other people because most people think in fragments, in segments, coupled with denial, forcing delay, and creating even more devastating problems. But you'll know that, because you've watched these situations as they've occurred again and again.

Second, you'll become a forecaster. This is the powerful part. While there is some truth to the observation that every scenario or pattern has its distinct differences, what is even more powerfully true is they also have enormously important, often crucial similarities. This being the case, you can make forecasts about strategies, approaches, and outcomes. And, while you'll be wrong at least 50% of the time, the magic of this insight is that you'll be right almost half the time. You'll be considered a veritable genius.

Pattern Examples

Both from management and communications perspectives, patterns provide powerful indications, which if ignored or carelessly addressed, can cause even the most crucial strategic intentions to fail, come apart, or cause even more problems. Even the most adverse of circumstances and the worst of surprises have recognizable elements and reasonably similar event sequences. Here are some examples.

Corporate Succession

The shorter the period of time between the publicly announced end of one leader's tenure to the succession of the next, the more likely it is that what is planned will actually occur. This is the pattern of success. The pattern of failure is when the current chairman announces their intention to retire 24–30 months out, names a successor, and then spends the remainder of the term of office trying to establish his/her immortality, build their legacy, and torpedo whatever it is the incoming successor might plan to accomplish. Such successions rarely succeed.

Corporate Restructuring

Often announced with big ballyhoo, projections of substantial cost savings, and perhaps even some new directions, restructurings frequently are accompanied by substantial cuts in employment combined with justifications and re-organizations. What is less often reported is that the proposed savings are more than consumed by the incredible cost of laying off hundreds, perhaps thousands of individuals. The turmoil caused by restructuring is often so destructive that key people, who were essential to the success of the fundamental concept, leave. The cycle repeats itself, usually within a few months or years. Most restructures fail in most respects.

Mergers and Acquisitions

Virtually all mergers and acquisitions are takeovers in one respect or another. If you've been on the side with less than 51% equity, even though the merger or acquisition was described as a "merger of equals" or "the perfect combination of two great companies," you know firsthand that it really was a takeover. The acquired company goes through a pattern of paralysis, loss of momentum, and loss of key people while everyone waits for the plan to be announced and implemented. Ironically, similar patterns are occurring in the acquiring company.

While there is eagerness to get on with the job and absorb the acquired institution, room has to be made, at least temporarily, for some key executives and officers from the acquired firm. Even though everyone's life is in total chaos, this is supposed to send a positive signal that keeps folks working and producing, at least until everyone discovers that there is no real plan.

Lots of paper may have changed hands, but the deal takes longer than planned to finalize and looks quite different from that originally envisioned. By the time things are ultimately squared away, the really valuable people in the acquired firm are beginning to execute their departure strategies, while many others are simply cut.

There never is a really well thought out integration approach, plan, or process. Some deals never come together, yet enormous damage is done.

There is often such pressure put on by the CEOs of the two major players to do the deal that rigorous analysis is actually avoided. Betting the entire business is one of the most exciting games top executives ever get to play.

Once set in motion, only extraordinary events (internally or externally), or a marketplace or governmental intervention can stop these deals from going forward. This is another crucial reason why virtually all acquisitions and mergers fail in most respects, except for those individuals who always benefit and become extremely wealthy as a result.

The Plant Shutdown

In the typical scenario, the decision to close a plant and reduce operations is "secretly" made by a small group of executives and then shared with a larger working group within a day or so. The target date is set for 60–90 days in the future (sometimes it is 3–4 times this long) so that "preparations" can be made internally to manage the process, and for compliance with various local, state, and federal laws and regulations.

Naturally, as the "secret" plan proceeds, word and rumors leak out (sometimes within hours of the original decision). Rumors of the shutdown plans often cause sudden and powerful increases in productivity and quality at the affected facility. The announcement is finally made (it may have been delayed two or three times due to "corporate scheduling"). Everyone in the affected facility is totally puzzled by the decision because they have been performing so well that, "Certainly someone would have noticed this by now." The decision is firm; the plant is scheduled for closing.

The unions announce that they and their international parent are working with a Wall Street investment banker to find a white knight to purchase the facility from the parent company. Failing that, the group will attempt an employee buyout in the hope that they can operate the facility themselves. High work quality and productivity continue, yet the parent company's decision remains firm. No buyers are found. The plant ultimately, belatedly, closes.

Exposure Management and Issue Surveillance

Exposure Management and Issue Surveillance is the purposeful monitoring of key corporate exposure sources and issues.

As noted in Chapter 2, the filtration of information gets so severe as it nears the top of an organization that most senior executives, especially the CEO, feel that what they receive is strained, refined, and drained of key information. One of the Trusted Strategic Advisor's most important roles is making certain that crucial information makes it to the top very promptly. Jim's description for this process is issue surveillance and exposure management.

The goals of exposure management and issue surveillance are to:

- Alert the top manager to possible threats and opportunities.
- Anticipate the organization's planned and unplanned visibility, internally and externally.
- Prepare management to act promptly, conclusively, and pragmatically.
- Work preemptively to mitigate and perhaps eliminate potential problems and threats.
- Estimate the potential organizational impact and exposure from threats, opportunities, and other circumstances.

This information is provided to the CEO in just two pages. These reports are so valuable that distribution is only at the discretion of the CEO.

Here is an example of a structure of Exposure Management and Issue Surveillance

Phase I: Identify Corporate Exposure Sources/Issues/Threats

In Part A there are major categories of threats and circumstances ranging from labor negotiations through site-specific issues, even executive speeches and key public appearances. Each of these elements, the list is customized to fit the organization involved, is scored to reflect its level of exposure threat to the organization.

In Part B, Impact Forecasting, specific areas of threat are scored, for their impact on the organization, should they occur.

As Phase I is completed, the scores of each item are tabulated and the three with the highest scores are then placed in the Response Priorities box under Phase II.

Phase II: Response Priorities

The purpose of this section is to highlight the highest scoring threat circumstances from Phase I and to prioritize them even further to determine where the highest level of management needs to be. This handful of key threats is sent to management for consideration and evaluation for preemptive work or planning.

Phase III: Limited Distribution of Confidential Exposure Reports

This section describes the policy and procedure with respect to these highly valuable and often highly inflammatory reports. As you can see, distribution is restricted and carefully controlled.

Phase IV: Quarterly Exposure Review Meetings

This part of the process is where management discloses its exposure surveillance results and works with others at very high levels in management to assure that the organization is prepared to eliminate or, at a minimum, compensate for, accommodate, or pre-empt the impact these potential threats might have (see Figure 8.1).

War Stories

Over the course of nearly 45 years of working in devastating civil, criminal, corporate, and government situations, Jim has amassed a rather amazing collection of scenarios. He calls them "war stories," and they occupy a significant portion of the file space in his office. Throughout most of his career, as urgent matters have arisen, he has established files for them. Mostly they contain important and relevant company documents, useful Tweets and web-based conversations, important news accounts, media articles, and commentary.

Should these situations arise again in his practice, he can instantly review relevant topical information and immediately begin to apply the lesson of patterns and forecastable circumstances to the questions my clients would be asking. He also creates files for scenarios he believes his clients will be asking about in the future. It happens nearly every day.

Fred, learning from Jim, began doing the same early in his career. Fred keeps an electronic file for dozens—now in the hundreds—of categories of issues, topics, kinds of crises, social issues, political processes, and experts. He adds to these regularly and can quickly find what he needs to be able to quickly come up the learning curve when an incident occurs.

Phase I
Identify Corporate Exposure Sources, Issues, and Threats

A. Identify Actions, Decisions, Events, and Activities to Monitor

Select those with special significance for impact and threat analysis in part B.

- ____ Activist demonstrations/threats
- ____ Angry neighbors
- ____ Competitive breakthroughs
- ____ Congressional testimony
- ____ Corporate liability
- ____ Criminal investigations
- ____ Employee unrest
- ____ Executive speeches
- ____ Government investigations
- ____ Hazardous waste
- ____ High-profile litigation
- ____ International sanctions
- ____ Key executive public appearances
- ____ Labor negotiations or actions
- ____ Major site-specific issues
- ____ Risk management plan (RMP)
- ____ Serious environmental cases
- ____ Significant news interviews
- ____ Superfund
- ____ Whistle-blowers
- ____

B. Forecast Impact and Threat Levels

1. Score each of these items on a scale of 1 to10, where 10 equals the highest level of impact.
2. Score each of these items on a scale of 1 to10, where 10 equals the highest degree of threat.

- __/__ Adverse court decisions
- __/__ Angry employees
- __/__ Anti-corporate action
- __/__ Congressional hearings
- __/__ Emergency potential
- __/__ Emerging issue or problem
- __/__ Exquisite threat
- __/__ Indictment of managers or employees
- __/__ Internal documents leaked
- __/__ Major management decisions
- __/__ Major media story
- __/__ Plant closing
- __/__ Product problems
- __/__ Prosecution
- __/__ Protestors
- __/__ Regulatory problems
- __/__ Takeovers
- __/__ Whistle-blowers
- __/__ ____________________

Phase II
Compute Response Priorities

Add the impact and threat numbers from phase I together to arrive at a combined score. List up to five items with the highest scores here, in descending order. These are your highest-priority issues for exposure management, surveillance, and readiness activity.

1. ____________
2. ____________
3. ____________
4. ____________
5. ____________

Phase III
Issue Confidential Exposure Reports

Write a synopsis for each of the issues or threats listed in phase II. Each synopsis should explore why the issue or threat is of utmost importance to the organization, the specific impact to be expected, and the consequences of failing to be ready.

• Number all copies • Prohibit any duplication or faxing • Collect copies after 72 hours • Revise surveillance and exposure goals and adjust readiness plans to reflect new information and current situation

Phase IV
Meet Quarterly for Exposure Review

• Identify new vulnerabilities • Eliminate old vulnerabilities • Provide feedback for revisions to response plan

Figure 8.1 Exposure Management and Surveillance Process

Scenario and pattern sensitivity is a state of mind and a discipline one chooses to acquire and use. The benefits are extraordinary. We have literally hundreds and hundreds of scenario files that we have been involved with or interested in throughout our careers.

Following is a partial list of the scenarios Jim has on file. The benefits are extraordinary.

Sample List from Jim's War Story Index

A

- Above-ground storage (nuclear fuel)
- Academic fraud
- Accidents
- Acquisitions
- Activist action
- Acts of God
- Adversarial interviews
- Adverse government action
- Adverse investigations
- Agency guidance
- AIDS
- Air quality violations
- Aircraft crashes
- Ambush interviews
- Analysts' presentations
- Angry neighbors
- Animal rights
- Annual meetings
- Anonymous accusers
- Anti-corporate activism
- Arsenic contamination
- Asbestos
- Attack sites

Keep in mind that our careers have been devoted to dealing mostly with the extraordinarily bad news of organizations, leaders, and institutions. Your list of scenarios, patterns, and topics of interest will conform, of course, to your own personal sphere of influence, current activities, and curiosity.

The Lessons of Pattern/Scenario Awareness

What can pattern analysis and scenario awareness accomplish? Here are five of the most crucial lessons:

Lesson #1: Patterns Are the Foundation of Strategy and Are What Make the Strategist an Intelligent Forecaster

Remember also that scenario planning and pattern analysis is a widely accepted management tool. The boss will be ready for and feel right at home having you walk him through scenarios and the potential benefits of understanding in advance what can happen. As we have emphasized throughout this book, leadership always benefits from useful, sensible suggestions about what the next steps or increments might be. This is among the greatest contributions Trusted Strategic Advisors can make. Pattern analysis is another key tool for advising the boss on what to do next.

Lesson #2: "War story" Files Are One Tool Advisors Can Use to Help the Boss Better Understand a Situation and All Its Ramifications as a Pattern of Events Unfolds

People often see an event or situation in isolation, or see only a small portion of it, missing its full scope. War story files can be put to use at a moment's notice to reveal the big picture and provide a basis for forecasting behaviors of key players.

Recently Jim received a call from someone who told him that he had been referred by their legal counsel. A story was about to appear in the newspaper about a senior executive about to be sued for sexual harassment. He wanted to know what to do. Having been through several cases, Jim was able to ask him crucial questions from the start.

"How many executives are involved?" was the first. "Just the one," he said, "and it's going to be a very high-profile situation." Jim's comment was that it's always more than just a single executive, and that it would be a very high-profile situation. Even if only one was engaged in actual harassment, other executives and managers were no doubt aware of this behavior and allowed it to occur. Those names would surface and the behavior of those executives and managers would be called into question.

"How many women are involved?" was the next. "Just the one," he answered tentatively. Jim commented that there has to be more than one. The pattern here is that this behavior involves multiple assaults on multiple individuals.

"Have you located previous female employees to determine why they left, what was said, and what is known about this individual's behavior?" was the third. "These women, while not speaking now due to shame, fear, or embarrassment will come forward as the story unfolds. Find out how many women are involved." Then he asked Jim, "Who have you been talking to?" Jim honestly answered, "No one, but what I'm telling you is the pattern of these events." This organization also tends to think that Jim is a genius.

Fred had a similar interaction. Just before Christmas one year he got a call from the general counsel of the US subsidiary of a large European bank. The bank was not at the time a client, but the general counsel had gotten Fred's name from his outside law firm.

He told Fred that the CEO of the US subsidiary had just been arrested for embezzlement of bank funds, which was about to be made public. The general counsel's question: Should we cancel the Christmas party scheduled for the next day? Fred dealt with the question of the party (answer: It depends . . .) but asked the general counsel a number of other questions. Have you done your own investigation? Have you looked for misconduct beyond the embezzlement? Have you notified your US regulators who supervise your operations in this country?

Fred became alarmed by the apparently casual attitude the general counsel was taking. Fred advised him to do three things: (1) Immediately hire the best financially sophisticated criminal defense law firm. (2) That very day, have the law firm contact the US regulatory authorities that regulate the bank and notify them of the arrest of the US CEO, before that arrest is made public. (3) Either through that law firm or directly, hire a private investigations firm to explore whether the US CEO might have engaged in other misconduct.

A week later the general counsel called Fred. He thanked him for the advice. He said that the regulators expressed great confidence in the bank for having notified them the same day as the arrest. He also said that when investigators visited the US CEO's summer home, they discovered dozens of pieces from the bank's corporate art collection hanging in that home. There was no record of those pieces having been removed from the corporate art collection. In other words, the art was stolen too. He asked, "How did you know to advise me about other misconduct?" Fred replied, "These things tend to follow common patterns."

Lesson #3: Preemptively Translate Relevant Patterns and Problems into Useful Strategic Tools Management Can Use Before Problems Occur

Maximize the value both of your "war stories" collections and your constant scanning of the issues and circumstances happening to other similar organizations. Select the most damaging, dangerous, or de-stabilizing situations, then translate them into hypothetical scenarios for your company or organization.

Here's an example: Suppose your company has manufacturing and distribution operations in a variety of locations in various towns and cities, large and small, all across the United States. However, most of your chemical treatment activities and heavy industry processes are located primarily in what are considered lower income, even poor areas.

You could someday be the subject of litigation or government action involving "environmental racism." If you were to search online for the terms "environmental racism" or "environmental justice," you'd come across the Environmental Protection Agency's (EPA) website (www.epa.gov) very quickly. If you search the site for "environmental justice," you'd find dozens of links about what the agency is doing to on environmental justice. One is a 2020 announcement by the EPA that it is partnering with the Department of Justice on more aggressive enforcement of environmental injustice. Within less than an hour, and even before you seriously reviewed your findings, you could be extraordinarily knowledgeable on this subject from very important sources, and have one or two brief case studies to back up your impressions, early information, and initial thoughts and recommendations.

Remember, the strategist's job is to provide an adequate explanation for the circumstance being discussed, described, debated, or deliberated; to understand and relate the nature of the threat or opportunity; to provide several options for management to consider and a recommendation for a particular approach complete with a brief analysis of the negative unintended consequences that could result from the various approaches.

Lesson #4: Focus Most of Your Work on Non-Operating Scenarios

Ninety-five percent of the problems that affect most organizations come directly from day-to-day operations. These are the areas in which there is significant resident expertise. The strategist looks at the other 5%, those non-operating circumstances that present the greatest threat to organizational stability, reputation, and market share and cause damage that is difficult to repair. Managements tend to be at their weakest in responding to non-operating problems.

The reason non-operating problems are so difficult for management to cope with is that they are rarely taught in business school. (Note: Fred does teach these in his crisis management seminar in the Executive MBA program in New York University's Stern School of Business.) These situations are often highly emotional, therefore, irrational, immeasurable, and embarrassing or humiliating besides.

Examples of non-operating problems include extortion, criminal litigation, employee or community violence, harassment, bullying or assault, activist attacks, attacks by determined adversaries, embarrassing or aggravating situations and allegations, extensive performance criticism, and shareholder activism. When these non-operating problems are poorly anticipated and handled, they cause the greatest damage to reputation and the greatest threat to the survival of CEOs. When there are victims, these highly emotionalized situations require special knowledge and expertise, but they also conform to recognizable patterns that can aid in the productive resolution of these situations.

Lesson #5: Talking Patterns Is Often a Powerful Way to Be Memorable

As we noted in Chapter 5, to have impact as a strategic advisor, what you say needs to be memorable. A number of years ago Jim was working with a small privately owned timber harvesting company in northern California. It was a highly controversial operation receiving significant negative visibility on a global scale. When the owners of this operation first called Jim, they told him they had the best intentions and wanted to make this operation a state-of-the-art, environmentally sustainable laboratory for forestry practices. They then mentioned that despite their good intentions and financial and philosophical ability to execute on their vision, they had terribly underestimated the negative reaction of a whole host of groups to their decision. So their question was very simple, "What do we do now?"

Jim immediately said, "Sell the property . . . this afternoon [it was July 4, 1998]." They didn't laugh. So Jim said, "No, seriously, sell the property this afternoon. Why do you need all the agony, grief, and embarrassment, or humiliation such a business and project will bring to you, and in fact probably already has?" Their answer was the same as before. They had the highest of motives in mind and they wanted to try to make the venture a success.

Jim went on to describe what they would in all likelihood experience, how difficult it would be, and the four things they really had to be ready for. First, they had to be willing to sacrifice much of their substantial wealth to counteract the enormous amount of anti-corporate activism that would be launched against them from many parts of the world. Second, they had to have the stomach for what was going to happen to each one of them—individually, their families, their other businesses, and their relatives. It would be a constant stream of gossip, fabrication, and sensationalism. Third, it was likely that the most highly visible among them, as well as the richest, would be singled out for special public naming and shaming, and that this is a part of the pattern of attack used by those who oppose them and others in similar situations. Fourth, and the concept toughest of all to internalize, is that this sort of behavior would in all likelihood continue for as long as they owned and worked the property. No matter how much they spent, how successful they were in habitat restoration, saving the salmon, rebuilding the forest floors, and other ecologically important behaviors and activities, they would likely be in the doghouse in a high-profile way with some people, advocacy groups, politicians, from nearby residents, and some cases, people throughout the world.

At the end of that phone call they thanked Jim for providing such a candid and lucid description of where they had been as well as where they were likely to be going.

They retained the business, have made it into one of the more prominent model forestry operations in America, one used as a best practices example by every major environmental group in the United States and abroad. And, their nickname for Jim alternates between "Joda" and "Dumbledore." Whenever they speak to him, they expect to hear about their future.

Can You Recognize What's Coming Next?

One of the most critical tasks of a trusted advisor is to help the leader figure out what to do next. Understanding the power of patterns can help you do that, because patterns can often be used to forecast what is going to happen next. We all tend to think we are unique, our situation special, our challenges exceptional.

Jim's and Fred's careers are a testament to the fallacy of this kind of thinking. In fact, we been advisors through all these years and have gone through so many different mostly adverse scenarios with organizations and leadership, with many of the smartest, best, and most leading-edge organizations on the planet. Still, it's crucial for us remember that no matter how hard we study the past, prevention of similar future mishaps is an erroneous mission.

The reason we so carefully need to study past circumstances is so that we will be prepared to deal with them when they occur once again, and then again, and then again.

Do you have the discipline necessary to collect and organize stories, reports, and case histories of a wide variety of events, companies, people, and situations? Will you spend the time to analyze structures, timelines, variables, and key decision-points? Can you keep it up year after year? Begin collecting your war stories now. At first, you will be unlikely to see patterns. But over time, you will. And you will be amazed at how people will seek you out, thinking you can see the future. Of course, what you will really be seeing are patterns. As Peter F. Drucker, who saw many trends emerging years before anyone else, once said, "I never predict. I simply look out the window and see what is visible but not yet seen."[1]

9 Advise Constructively

Chapter Outline

How to structure advice so that you are clearly understood and the boss can act on your advice, pitfalls to giving advice, strategies and techniques to help you structure advice and three strategic tools to use.

How to Deliver Powerful, Important, and Meaningful Advice

Your Operational Decision-Making

Most staff advisors, early on, tend to give advice in the context of their staff function or personal area of expertise. The problem is staff thinking and decision-making are quite different from operational thinking and decision-making. Operational executives tend to be process thinkers. Successfully providing useable advice to operating executives requires a change in thinking and style on the part of the Trusted Strategic Advisor. The goal of this change is to align giving advice with the thinking patterns and decision-making habits of operating executives. As Fred preaches, you can't move people if you don't meet them where they are. And for the trusted advisor it is crucial that they think and communicate in a simpler structured and process-driven format. This ensures senior executives will "get it" faster.

When the solution proposed is bold, obvious common sense, absolutely applicable, or brilliant and creative, managers will absorb advice better if it fits into their processing approach, builds on their intuitive skills and experience, and allows them to decide faster.

The Three-Minute Drill

That's the Three-Minute Drill in a nutshell. When Jim learned this approach, it was referred to as the "Concept of Completed Action," which he learned as President of the ExecuCom Division of Brum and Anderson, a Minneapolis Public Relations firm. After some experimentation, Jim re-named the process "The Three-Minute Drill" as we'll explain in a few minutes. The value of this structured thinking and presentation approach has been a crucial ingredient in Jim's success. Fred adopted this approach early in his career and has taught it to many students and clients, and it too has been a crucial ingredient to his success.

Brevity is crucial to avoid the urge to overtalk. Brevity is important because concentrated, well-structured information presented verbally or in writing is powerful and more likely to be assimilated and owned by others. Most critical decisions are made based on experience, the leader's intuition, plus facts and information recently harvested through verbal interaction with colleagues and advisors in very short spans of time. The challenge is always to provide essential information to enable executives to know what to do next. And to do it in a way that values the executive's time.

The Six Active Elements of the Three-Minute Drill (450 Words)

The Three-Minute Drill is a time-driven approach to presenting recommendations. The three minutes refers to the amount of time you're likely to have with a senior decision-maker before that decision-maker becomes distracted, bored, or lost. The drill is structured in six steps that impose a useful, sensible, management decision-making structure:

Step 1. Situation/Introduction (60 words): A brief description of the nature of the issue, problem, or situation that requires decision, action, or study. This is the factual basis, "Here's where we are now, and here's what we know."

Step 2. Analysis/Assumptions (60 words): A brief description of the significance of the situation, what its implications are, and how it threatens or presents an opportunity to the organization, or individual leader. Include the one or two key assumptions that validate the analysis. "Here's why it matters." It includes a brief but clear description of the risks or opportunities involved.

Managers always need to know the why, but briefly with essential details. They are also interested in the intelligence you have gathered or know about that supports your analysis and assumptions.

Step 3. The Goal (60 words): The desired outcome. A clear, concise statement of the task to be accomplished (sometimes the reason or purpose for accomplishing it) or the target to be reached and why. "This is where we are headed." If the significance in Step 2 is a risk or threat, then the goal in Step 3 is the mitigation of that risk or threat. If the significance is an opportunity, then the goal is to realize that opportunity.

Goals keep everyone focused. Useful goals are understandable, achievable, brief, positive, and time/deadline sensitive. And more importantly, the boss will want the payoff previewed early.

Step 4. Options/Outcomes (150 words): Provide at least three response options to address the situation as presented and analyzed. For each option, be prepared to address the foreseeable intended and unintended outcomes.

Option one is to do nothing or nothing out of the ordinary (the 0% solution); list the foreseeable consequences, both intended and unintended.

Option two is to do something modest (the 100% solution); list the foreseeable consequences, both intended and unintended.

Option three is to do something more (the 125% solution); list the foreseeable consequences, both intended and unintended.

Step 5. Recommendation (60 words): This is calling out the choice you would make among the options you presented. The recommendation is usually selected on the basis of which option will cause the least number of unintended negative consequences. And here is where you can briefly describe how to operationalize that option.

This is where you earn your paycheck. The boss will always want to know what you would do if you were in his/her shoes. Be prepared to choose one of the options proposed, and to defend it.

Many times we have heard advisors offer reasonable options, but when the boss ultimately asks the question, "What is the first thing I should do," or "What are the next steps," or "Of the three recommendations, which would you choose and why," far too often the response from the proposer, "Gee, boss, that's a good question and I need to think about that." This response puts an end to the advisor's usefulness in the discussion, at least in this round, and may undercut later advice.

Be ready with a recommendation and supporting information every time.

Step 6. Justification (60 words): These are the reactions or circumstances that could arise resulting from the options you suggested. Every management decision or action has intended and unintended consequences that can be forecast. Consequences can sabotage an otherwise useful strategy.

When we think of consequences and strategy, we generally think of trying to identify the solution option with the least number of negative intended or unintended consequences.

One of the core disciplines here is to never justify the decision using the vocabulary of personal preference—"I prefer this one"—or of intuition—"I really feel we should do this one." Rather, always use the vocabulary of the outcomes. "Of the three alternatives, this is the one with be best set of outcomes."

The Options

Jim's preference, as a strategist, is to talk about doing nothing before anyone else does. Jim's experience is that when the lawyers talk about doing nothing, the discussion sometimes ends right at that point. The discussion only resumes when some catastrophic development or unexpected adverse situation occurs. As a strategist, his sense is that he's often in the best position to discuss the impacts and costs of doing nothing better than any other staff function. Certainly, human resources, finance, strategic planning, security, and IT can also address the circumstance, but on issues that matter, where there are victims and serious visibility risks, doing nothing can be extremely costly. This option needs to be discussed and debated as a valid, serious strategy.

The option to do something is crucial. Most problems, although benefiting from some initial lack of action, do require some input of energy, resources, talent, and decision-making to be resolved. Having an action recommendation assists the boss in that crucial area called "what to do next."

Doing something more is important to resolving problems, especially those that are disturbing, stressful, or destructive to an organization, may require more than a minimally adequate response. Doing something more means going beyond meeting the letter of the law or the minimum and taking additional steps that will further enhance the organization's reputation, assist those adversely affected, or repair a previous mistake. This approach is often the difference between a leadership solution and a manager's solution, which only addresses the known visible elements of a given situation.

Fred has used the Three-Minute Drill consistently since he first learned it from Jim. More significantly, Fred has taught the Three-Minute Drill for decades, to graduate students, to individual clients, and to groups of clients. Invariably, clients and students report—even many years later—that using this method was transformational, to them in their careers and to their organizations. Some clients have asked Fred to teach the Three-Minute Drill to whole departments and teams, so that they have a common approach to understanding problems, opportunities, and ways to influence leaders' decisions.

Death by Question, Surviving the Advice-Giving Gauntlet

The corporate execution method for big ideas is "Death by Question," usually at the hands of other staff functions. You have a wonderful idea for solving a serious corporate problem. Your idea is innovative, interesting, and somewhat different from the usual approaches. Rather than shooting your idea down by saying it won't work, it's not possible, it doesn't fit the culture, other negatives, shooting down the idea begins with a series of questions.

- "Have you run this by finance to determine the fiscal impact?" You probably haven't, which means your idea is now bleeding from a serious wound. Then comes killer question two,
- "Has human resources had a chance to review the impact on employees, service levels, and local operating structures?" It's another bullet, of slightly larger caliber. But they've saved the best and biggest bullet for last,
- "If you were given the go-ahead with your proposal, could you finance it completely out of your own budget this year?" Well, by now it feels like your idea is lying in a bloody puddle on the floor, and you are out of arguments and out of the game.

The concept of options is powerful because it can give you the power to withstand Death by Question. You may be shot down on one part of your idea, perhaps even a good part of the second concept, but it's rare that even a large group can shoot down three suggestions. Some fragment of your thinking is going to remain on the table. This means you will undoubtedly be in the room through the entire discussion.

Keep in mind, the ultimate decision may hardly resemble anything that you proposed, but as a Trusted Strategic Advisor, you're still there, you're still in the game, you're still ready to offer additional options beyond the first set. This is one of the crucial values the Trusted Strategic Advisor provides—a useful, restrained, but critical attitude that provides ideas for tomorrow and helps move whole issues and circumstances to new levels of understanding and resolution.

Controlling the Choice of Options

Sometimes Jim is asked, "What if there is only one appropriate action for the boss to take?" His response: "Everyone knows it, even the boss knows it, but there's resistance. Would it be possible to use this technique so that after you discuss doing nothing, you offered something you know the boss should do, and then something so ridiculous that the boss's choice is clearly obvious?" Jim's experience has been that, frankly, the more outlandish the suggestion you make is, the more likely it is that the boss will select it. And, of course, because you suggested it, you'll be put in charge of making it work. This is a very risky strategy. Let the process of executive decision-making play out. Offer options that are useful, sensible, and appropriate; options you can ethically and professionally execute. Help the process of decision-making move ahead through your remaining analysis and suggestions.

It's the boss's career. The ultimate decision is up to the boss. Whatever the boss chooses, you'll be there to help and advise.

Learn and Use This Management Decision-Making Structure

Each of the six management decision-making components just discussed has three powerful common elements.

Factual Basis

What is actually known, can be counted on, trusted, seen, or measured. In the early stages of change, important situations are so often under-factualized that logical decision-making seems difficult, if not impossible. As you think about giving advice in this format, facts matter. Examples will help. But management will need to see sufficient information to provide measurable or conclusive evidence of progress.

Real-Time

On issues that matter, ideally the gap in time between decision and action is a very small or short. The larger the time separation between decision and action, the greater the likelihood that significant factual change may make a portion or all of the action decisions faulty, or at least less than optimum.

Outcome Focus

Strategic decision-making is always about moving toward the future. The past can only be re-imagined, rewritten, and reinterpreted. It is what it was. Focusing on outcomes helps set the past aside and deal in terms of tomorrow. This is the destiny-driven approach.

This is a strategic approach. It leads to productive, focused decision-making. Use it and you'll get to help managers at every level make better strategic decisions. In fact, use this approach and you will find yourself being called in earlier and asked to stay longer.

Worksheet 9.1, The Three-Minute Drill, fulfills two important functions. It's a guided approach through the process of thinking and developing this technique. Keep in mind the word counts and the purpose for each of the six elements. You can use this format on your computer or as a handwritten form and worksheet you bring to meetings to develop options on the spot.

Worksheet 9.1 Three-Minute Drill Worksheet

Issue, Question, Situation ______________________________

A declaration of the topic to be discussed.

1. **Situation**
(60 Words)
A brief description of the nature of the issue, problem, or situation that requires decision, action, or study—"This is the subject and here's what we know now."

2. **Analysis/Assumptions**
(60 Words)
A description of what the situation means, what its implications are, the significance of the risks the situation represents, and how it threatens or presents an opportunity to the organization. "Here's why it matters."

3. **Goal**

(60 Words)
A clear, concise statement of the task to be accomplished (sometimes the reason or purpose for accomplishing it), the target to be reached, the mitigation of the identified risks, and realization of identified opportunities. It is "Our destination."

4. **Options**

(150 Words)
Provide at least three response options for the situation as presented and analyzed.
For each, include foreseeable intended and unintended outcomes.

Options:

1. Do nothing; foreseeable intended and unintended outcomes.
2. Do something; foreseeable intended and unintended outcomes.
3. Do something more; foreseeable intended and unintended outcomes.

    1.
    2.
    3.

(*continued*)

5. **Recommendation**
(60 Words)
Be prepared to explain the choice you would make among the options presented. And to briefly summarize how to operationalize that choice: "The next steps."

6. **Justification**
(60 Words)
The recommendation is selected on the basis of outcomes: the recommended option will cause the least number of negative unintended consequences.

Worksheet 9.2, the Best Option Process Worksheet, is a different format for beginning to develop your Three-Minute Drill if you're going through this process as a small or large group. The worksheet is designed more as a discussion support template. Here again, it's designed to help structure, contain, and facilitate the process of developing options and the related information.

This worksheet is designed to capture the Three-Minute Drill approach. The total amount of time to present concepts to management, in the order shown in the worksheet, should be approximately three minutes speaking time, or 450 words or less. Always maximize the value of time spent with executives, from their perspective.

Worksheet 9.2 Best Option Process Worksheet

Date:______________

Problem: Describe clearly, directly, and briefly.

____

____

Urgency: Why now; the risks or opportunities.

(60 Words)

____

____

Outcome Desired: What's the goal: mitigation of the risks or realization of the opportunity.

____

____

Solution Options: Identify the alternatives; for each, the foreseeable outcomes.

1. ____
____
2. ____
____
3. ____
____

Best Option: Recommend the first-choice action (also indicate the second-best option).

____

____

Reasons (Consequences): Justify your choice: indicate the consequences avoided and achieved.

1. ____
____
2. ____
____

The message of both Worksheet 9.1 and Worksheet 9.2 is that, at the rate of 450 words per recommendation, you're talking to time and should be able to get your recommendations on one side of one sheet of paper. This is always an excellent strategy when providing written materials you want your boss to act upon.

More Strategic Advice-Giving Tools

To supplement the Concept of Completed Action as just explained and to help give additional information in a management context, there are three additional important tools the advisor might choose to use:

Timelines

One of the most strategic documents for making recommendation is the timeline, driven by the calendar, or a clock, depending on the timeframes being considered. We've made the point time and again that management is about tomorrow. Any recommendations that fit in the sequence of getting things done, making decisions, or choosing alternatives are more important than other activities. The timeline concept can accommodate a variety of different activities all moving forward at the same time, but at different velocities.

For example, when locating or siting a new building, plant, or branch office, there can be literally dozens of timelines at work and interacting with each other. The list would include design and architecture, site acquisition and public permit acquisition; public affairs and policy chains, planning and communications; legal and regulatory issues, permissions, oversight, and restrictions; recruiting locally for available positions; occupancy checklists and requirements—you get the idea.

Another value of timelines is that if one element of a particular schedule of activities slips, slides, is eliminated, or occurs early, it is easy to adjust the timeline, and the overall thinking and strategy are less affected, if at all.

Priorities

Another extremely helpful technique is to prioritize actions, events, decisions, and outcomes. Virtually any list of activities, or ideas and concepts that is prioritized is strategically helpful. Part of being a strategic advisor is about establishing priorities and helping the boss know what to do next and what the range of options to accomplish the next steps happen to be.

Helping the boss set priorities is helping set the agenda for the entire organization. This is a powerful activity for any advisor.

Flowcharts

Another powerful communication technique for advisors is the flowchart. There are many different varies of flowcharts, but the more complex an idea, concept, or recommendation, the more valuable developing a prioritized picture of actions, steps, and decisions becomes.

Operations people are used to reading flowcharts as well as thinking in process terms.

Next time, rather than writing a complicated memo of recommendations, try drawing the recommendation as a sequence of events from beginning to end, designed as a picture of decisions and actions moving ahead in an organized, prioritized fashion.

A single flowchart, generally on one side of one sheet of paper, is worth at least a notebook full of words and tabs.

You can believe us when we tell you that using this technique will change your relationship with just about everyone, especially senior people. Most importantly, it will help you gain those things you treasure most as a Trusted Strategic Advisor, acceptance, access, impact, inclusion, influence, and respect. We'd like to hear from you about your experience as you learn to use The Three-Minute Drill.

10 Show the Boss How to Use Your Advice

Chapter Outline

Teach the boss how to take and to use your advice, four approaches to providing constructive advice, seven elements of effective advice, and how to assess your daily performance. Work to be a wise advice giver.

In his groundbreaking book, *Taking Advice*, Dan Ciampa talks about the "attitudes and behaviors of great advice takers." Among the insights on this topic, Ciampa discusses the relationship that needs to be established between the boss and the trusted advisor. He talks about four behaviors bosses tend to look for: practicality, added value, dependability, and commitment.

He actually refers to these as relationship tests because both the advisor and the leader must pass them together.

Practicality, according to Ciampa, puts the advisor in a position to give useful, doable, achievable, advice because instructions, goals, and expected behaviors are clear.

The added-value test refers to the dialogue between the advisor and the leader. This test is passed if "at the end of each substantive meeting the leader knows something more valuable than they did before, or is more clear-headed about how to proceed."[1]

The third test is dependability. It's essentially the "can I trust this person" question. Does the advisor spontaneously provide useful, helpful information as expected, and is the leader forthcoming at the same time, responsive to the advice being given in a tone that it respectful and helpful?

The fourth test, commitment, is in relation to the leader-advisor relationship. According to Ciampa the defining questions from the boss's perspective are:

1. Does the advisor genuinely seem interested in the kinds of problems I have?
2. Does the advisor seem to care about my success?

Clearly, if the answer to these questions is yes, a successful relationship is more likely to develop and the leader is likely to become a better advice taker.

But there are other habits and behaviors of trusted advisors that foster, nurture, and maintain this spirit of collaborative dialoguing, resulting in actions and behaviors on the part of leaders that reflect the value of the shared relationship. Once a Trusted Strategic Advisor proves their dependability, the first imperative is to teach clients how to use the advice they are given.

Giving Constructive Advice

Being constructive has a special meaning when it comes to being a Trusted Strategic Advisor. It means avoiding, in fact eliminating, the use of criticism as an advisory technique. Replace that negative approach by always providing helpful, positive assistance.

But being constructive is actually even deeper and broader than that. One of the ingredients of genuine leadership is the ability to hear many voices; then to choose the most interesting, helpful, important, or powerful elements of those voices and to fashion a new structure of ideas, decisions, and actions. It has struck Jim over the years that the "attitude" of the information received determines how useful or acceptable it will be in resolving issues and helping move toward the future. One of the key disciplines of a successful advisor is the ability to provide information with the right tone, the right structure, and the right intention.

Sharing your intentions with those you counsel is also essential to your success. Rather than waiting for your client to notice, take the time to explain the what, why, how, when, and where of your advice style, and the techniques you use.

Constructive approaches have four elements.

Goal Focus

As Stephen Covey would say, plan with the end it mind, have a destination before you start the journey, and understand the outcome you seek to achieve before you begin. More good intentions perish on the rocks and shoals of unknown destinations than for almost any other reason. Goal focus tends to reduce the wandering generality tendency and force focus on more meaningful specifics, more meaningful calls to action that develop the desired outcomes. If the goal is missing, you and the boss are going nowhere.

Long-Term Thinking

It's true, the vast majority of advice sought and given relates to matters occurring generally within a current budget or fiscal period. The strategic advisor's perspective is always to look at today's decisions in terms of their consequences on tomorrow. A wonderfully important achievement today may actually be somewhat cumbersome to explain in a future context when such activity can be viewed from an entirely different and perhaps negative perspective. Long-term thinking says, in some respects, everything we do today, that matters, affects tomorrow. We must at least think about those impacts and outcomes and advise more carefully today if we want to have better outcomes tomorrow.

Process Driven

This approach generally reflects the mentality and attitude of senior managers. They've learned that the best results come from processes, steps, parts, elements, phases, and ingredients that can be taught, replicated, evaluated, and help ensure a uniform level of quality in behavior, practice, and process outcomes.

Even the advice given has to be structured using a process-driven format, or it will be largely ignored, misunderstood, or disregarded.

Strategic Relevance

Among all the ingredients of being a Trusted Strategic Advisor, being strategic is the most challenging.

So often, staff functions have difficulty relating to corporate strategy. We talk a good game, even use a lot of management vocabulary, but our minds simply fail to function in a strategic way, and we produce advice that is too shallow, or only of limited use. To a certain extent, this is expected. Each staff function has its relevant applicability to achieving organizational or leadership goals. Yet, among the major lessons of the seven discipline approach that these disciplines aid the trusted advisor in maintaining a sense of management relevance.

Giving Advice Effectively

Another way of looking at helping those you advise actually utilize your advice is talking in ways that help ensure that they can and will listen. The six approaches suggested here help achieve this goal.

Be Positive

In business conversation, when someone says something with which there is disagreement, the response is often something like, "You're wrong," or "That's incorrect," or "You don't know what you're talking about," or "It's simply not done that way," or some similar negative approach. You may then explain what is correct or how you really do things, but your listener is still dealing with the insult of your negative language. This makes it almost impossible for him/her to hear your constructive language. Negative comments almost always put people on the defensive even though we have important, positive, constructive things to say.

Table 10.1 Bad News Eradicator Sample

Bad News Eradicator Sample	
Negative	***Positive***
"We don't do it that way."	"Here's the way we do it . . ."
"That's not our style."	"Here are important elements of our style . . ."
"The boss won't buy it."	"Here's what the boss has bought in the past; here's what they may buy in the future . . ."
"That's a lie."	"If you check your facts and assumptions you may come to a different conclusion." Or, "Using the same analysis we came up with a different, more positive result."

"The Bad News Eradicator" is a little exercise Jim does with clients in which he presents a list of common negative phrases and then turn them into positives. Table 10.1 demonstrates how this is done.

The lesson is this: Your use of negative language limits your relationship with other people. Eradicate or eliminate negative and emotional words and you become far more powerful and in control of almost any situation. Your positive approach blocks or defeats those who are negative. Most arguments, misunderstandings, confusion, and aggressive behavior are triggered by negative words, phrases, and attitudes. In situations of confrontation and controversy, at least one side of the argument needs the negativity of the other to continue operating effectively and pushing the argument forward. Eliminate that negative energy, and progress can actually be made, or a more peaceful resolution can be sought after.

Eliminate Criticism as a Coaching and Advising Practice

Using criticism as a teaching and change technique leads to very bad results. The people you advise are hurt or confused. Often negative advice leads to even more negative behavior. Constructive criticism is an oxymoron. Angry, negative language generates a future with angry, negative people. Positive outcomes require positive language.

Example: Recently a friend called Jim. She was in charge of evaluating the performance of the new minister in her church after a year's service. She put together a brief letter to members of the congregation asking that they provide some "constructive criticism" of the minister's performance. She mailed 700. She received more than 500 responses, each of which contained an average of three comments. Some contained even more.

The feedback was devastating. If you added up all of the criticisms, there was no way this minister could possibly continue in the job and survive emotionally. Most of the criticisms were negatives; many reflected individual misunderstandings; and virtually none reflected knowledge of the scope of the congregation's mission or the daily activities required of the minister as the congregation's leader. The criticisms boiled down to negative personal commentary.

Jim's friend's problem was, of course, that she had to share this information with the minister. If she didn't have something else worked out, he would undoubtedly resign. While the congregation really liked this man and wanted him to stay, not even a minister could withstand this level of personal criticism.

Jim told her about a lesson he learned early in his career from the late Chester Burger, who was America's most famous, beloved, and influential business communications consultant for many decades. As a communication consultant he faced similar situations inside corporations. His strategy, which Jim has followed for years, was to ask each client executive to make one positive constructive suggestion about what they might do to achieve the goals of the organization rather than using criticism of past performance as a technique. The application of this technique is incredibly powerful.

Ask anyone to criticize and critique your appearance, preparation, proposal, presentation, personality . . . anything, and you are guaranteed to get dozens of minor negative comments, most of which you couldn't use or implement even if you wanted to. Most critiques are designed to elicit negative, unhelpful information, are irritating, and often embarrassing.

My friend did go back and use this technique. She wrote a simple note to congregation members asking them to suggest up to three things the pastor could do in the next six to nine months to move the congregation into the future. Out of the 700-member congregation, she received 12 suggestions. Each was implementable and achievable within the next 30–90-day period.

My friend went back to the minister, in all honesty, and showed the first assessment from the congregation, but then showed the follow-up work.

The minister not only stayed, but implemented every suggestion in the first 90 days.

The lesson is this: We have the power to structure and control productive discussions and debate. If you want constructive results, seek and insist on constructive suggestions. There will be very few, but they will be useful. If you are constructive and seek positive, constructive suggestions, you automatically control and, therefore, powerfully manage how decisions are made.

Urge Prompt Action

Speed is the great detoxifier and emotion controller. Acting quickly defeats or preempts the actions of critics. Prompt apology can all but eliminate litigation. Speedy decisions and actions help you outrun the competition and those who love to live in the past. The longer it takes a senior manager or senior leaders to respond, the more complex the solution to the problem becomes. In this day and age, every leader, and certainly every trusted advisor, should be prepared for surprise to the point where they can avoid time-consuming meetings and delays by exercising pre-authorized responses to attacks, problems, instability, fear, mistakes, or errors.

Over the years we have learned that whether it's an activist group, angry employees, upset neighbors, or jealous competitors—the unwanted merger, the threat of litigation, legislation, or organization—who appear to be outsmarting us, the way to win, the way to move things forward, the way to stay in charge is to act now, and do it now . . . every time.

This often means making smaller decisions and acting on them more quickly:

- Answer it now. If there are questions, get the answers and get them now.
- Ask it now. Rather than waiting for someone else to ask the serious question, ask first to get the answer.
- Challenge it now. If it's wrong, correct it. If it's legitimate, act on it. If it's an alternative worth considering, decide and act.
- If you know it's going to be a problem, act now to eliminate the cause.
- Fix it now. If it's broken, move to repair it; if it's breaking down, move to shore it up.

The lesson is this: Those who act promptly, who do it now, are ahead of the competition and produce fewer new critics, enemies, and naysayers. Prompt action often foils the opposition's most carefully laid plans and can defeat almost any critic, while better controlling the situation.

The linear thinkers may criticize you for this, "Move that fast and you'll make more mistakes." Mistakes will be made anyway. Deferring them to some other time only delays success and makes them worse. Make the inevitable mistakes early. Fix them faster and move on more successfully. You'll just make different mistakes earlier. Jim would say, "Let's make tomorrow's mistakes yesterday and we'll be way ahead."

Focus on Outcomes

Always focus on a goal. Some time ago, Jim was deeply involved in negotiations between some powerful anti-corporate forces: groups of labor unions, church groups, and non-governmental organizations. The issues were extraordinarily compelling, in the news, divisive, and to some extent in the streets. The challenge was to find a way to sit down face-to-face, put these matters in some perspective, and develop a plan of action.

Fortunately, someone suggested that they meet with a minister in Brooklyn Heights, New York, just across the East River from Manhattan. He was reputed to have personal presence and an unusual strategy to manage such a politically charged confrontation. They met in the minister's living room in December. This huge, jovial man greeted the group warmly, asked them to sit down together in front of a roaring fire, listen to some music, and be quiet for a few minutes.

He then laid down just one ground rule for the day's work: the discussion was to be entirely outcome focused. This meant that whatever happened between us prior to entering his living room was out of bounds (disagreements, arguments, behaviors, truth, fiction, and lies). The past was completely off-limits to our current discussion. If this ground rule was a problem, he promised to end the discussions and bid us a pleasant day.

It's crucial to understand just how powerful this concept is. Fundamentally, it recognizes that everyone owns yesterday, last week, last month, and last year, from their own point of reference. That ownership is permanent. Even given a limitless amount of discussion, the past will remain as it was, owned by those who were there.

But no one owns the future—the next 15 minutes, the next day, the next week, the next month, the next year. Therefore, when we choose to be outcome-focused, we are choosing to enter, live, and build a future together.

Now back to Brooklyn Heights. Each time anyone began a discussion supported by something from the past, our host would halt the discussion and refocus it on tomorrow. It was tough for these real time adversaries to stick to the process, but by 4:30 that afternoon they had negotiated and signed a one-page agreement. Those who signed it, and the businesses and organizations they represented, lived by that agreement for years.

The lesson is this: Focus on tomorrow and take from yesterday only the positive, useful, constructive elements and ideas that can move the process forward, promptly. There will be very few, if any. Focusing on the future allows you to build tomorrow free of the problems misunderstandings, and crippling assumptions of the past.

Bonus lesson: Applying this single concept will substantially cut meeting and discussion time. A good portion of most meetings is spent explaining to those who weren't at the last meeting what went on and what has yet to be done. Then, it's necessary to re-explain again because some of those who attended the last meeting have a very different perception of what went on than you do. What little time remains is finally used to get something done and move ahead. Skip yesterday. Go to tomorrow and save tons of time.

Tomorrow can only start when today is over. Todays that are governed by yesterday only cause more problems and may even prevent a successful tomorrow. Outcome focus saves precious time, reduces mistakes and misunderstandings, and acts as a positive force for moving ahead.

You get to the future faster by starting there.

Be Carefully Reflective

In the previous chapter, we emphasized the importance of examining past patterns. Because patterns repeat themselves, they can lead to a powerful scenario planning process. How does that jibe with the advice to be goal oriented and always focus on tomorrow? The point is this: consult the past selectively and carefully, with a specific purpose—that being to strengthen your advice about the future. It can be useful to reflect on certain past situations and how others have dealt with similar issues.

Remember, the boss needs advice on what to do next. Seek only useful, positive lessons from the past, if you go there at all. Valuable positive lessons from the past are very rare. Studying the past to predict the future can be extremely risky. Looking backward, like walking backward, is the opposite of looking forward.

One of the silliest aphorisms one hears about the past is "Hindsight is 20/20." In our experience, foresight is almost always confused, mistaken, and flawed in many respects and needs to be reinterpreted constantly. Hindsight can't be 20/20 because foresight is always wrong.

Be an Incrementalist

An incrementalist strives for the successful forward step rather than the global solution. As mentioned, most bosses are skeptical of silver bullets, big ideas, and brilliant strategies. They realize that progress is actually made incrementally, often following established patterns of thinking and experience, after rigorous exploration and study, with a hint of intuition and strategic thinking. The incrementalist breaks problems into solvable parts and works to resolve each increment of the problem promptly.

Being an incrementalist actually prepares the leader and the organization to watch for and recognize big breakthroughs. Such breaks are as much a matter of luck as anything. Luck is limited. Luck actually comes most often to those who are relentlessly incremental in their personal progress every day. As Louis Pasteur so famously said, "Chance favors the prepared mind."

The most credible advisors are those who relentlessly and intentionally:

- Grow and learn every day.
- Help those they serve to achieve some positive incremental progress every single day.
- Identify and talk about those positive increments that they work with, supervise, or lead every day.
- Assess what they've learned, then teach those learnings to others.

Be Pragmatic

Your credibility rests more on what you are actually able to accomplish than on any series of goals or concepts you may choose to announce but only partially, or fail to, achieve. Pragmatic advisors focus on what's doable.

One of the more interesting stories about pragmatism appears in Jack Welch's book *Straight from the Gut*. He had just finished listening to nuclear engineers decide how they were going to begin selling three nuclear reactors per year in the United States and how this would save this General Electric division.

After listening for an hour, Welch thoughtfully responded that no matter how good the intentions were, nuclear reactors were not going to be sold again in the United States in their lifetime, that they needed to focus on something else, and perhaps servicing existing nuclear facilities would be a more pragmatic approach. GE became top in its category of servicing nuclear facilities. Mr. Welch was being a pragmatist.

The lesson is this: A pragmatist matches rhetoric with reality. Put yourself in the other person's shoes. See the world from their perspective. Help them achieve your goals by achieving a portion of their goals in ways they recognize, and from their own perspective. Dale Carnegie was right, "Help the other guy get what he wants, from his perspective; and he'll help you get what you want, from your perspective."

Pragmatism is saying and doing things that "make sense."

Advice Givers and Advice Takers

As you seek to give effective advice, it is useful to remember Dan Ciampa's point from the beginning of this chapter that both leaders and advisors must work to make the advising relationship effective. As Ciampa points out, effective leaders know how to solicit and take advice.

But sometimes bosses simply don't want to hear the advice they receive or resent being put in a position where they need to ask for advice. Since the business scandals of the early 2000s, CEOs are on the defensive because they are increasingly being measured on standards for which they haven't been trained, and never expected to be. They're being measured on their morality, their belief systems, their commitment to society, and to some degree on the perception of honesty and integrity they tend to convey. Public attitude surveys consistently demonstrate that the public is fed up with the apparent greed and amorality of corporate leadership. The more hard-bitten executives resent being given advice along these lines.

One of Jim's client companies some years ago was indicted for dozens of felonies, implicated in at least two deaths, and charged with conspiracy involving the alteration of medical products without FDA approval—criminal matters all. It took six years, but the matter finally came to trial, and the company pleaded guilty. Jim wrote the allocution statement for the CEO, who replaced the former CEO who was indicted, acquitted, and retired. In addition, Jim helped the law firm develop the plea agreement, and its very onerous restrictions and sanctions (the company paid what was at the time the highest fine ever levied by the government in an FDA product tampering case).

Jim was deeply involved in developing the company's code of conduct revisions, the integrity revisions, and some of the compliance standards and enforcement procedures. The law firm allowed him to present his own work in connection with theirs to senior management. The goal was to review the guidelines as laid out in the plea agreement, and, frankly, how the company was going to be operated for the foreseeable future.

When the presentation was finished and it was time for questions, the CEO of the company, who never really liked Jim anyway, said, "Lukaszewski, whenever you are around here, it seems a little bit like Sunday school." Jim's response was, "Well Bill, if my company just plead guilty to dozens of felonies, I think a little Sunday school might be in order." Everybody but Bill laughed. Ironically, Bill's term as CEO lasted only another eight months. Then he was gone. For many years, Jim continued as a consultant.

The lesson is that some bosses resent taking advice, even if they know they have to follow it. Sometimes a bad relationship cannot be fixed because of the boss's attitude. The onus of building a good relationship is, as Ciampa noted, a shared responsibility. You also need a leader who seeks advice in good faith. If the person you are advising avoids dealing in good faith, why would you want to stay?

Be a Wise Strategic Force

Giving advice effectively is a strategic force that helps drive individuals, organizations, cultures, and societies forward every day. The discipline of being intentionally constructive, with a relentlessly positive approach, helps those you advise be more receptive to the help you offer.

How will you know when you have become a strategic force as an advisor? Here are some indicators:

- You'll be invited to share your opinions at higher levels within your organization.
- As a matter of daily routine, you'll be able to articulate what is truly important, useful, and helpful to others.
- You'll notice that, from your perspective, you are doing more important things. You will move to more important work than you're currently doing.
- It may mean evaluating your current environment and determining whether or not you can become a leadership force within the situation in which you currently find yourself.

Your Daily Personal Self-Assessment

Leaders automatically tend to assess their own performance each day. They ask themselves several questions. This is a personal discipline that will ensure that even their most frustrating day is rewarding and important: As an advisor, you should ask the same questions:

- What did I learn today?
- How can I apply that learning to something I'm currently working on or something I want to work on?
- What did others learn from me today?
- How many times today did someone tell me they heard me quoted in a meeting they attended and people were inspired to move ahead?
- How or what have I improved in some way for someone else today?

PART III Conclusion

11 You Are the Table

Chapter Outline

The Table Is a Myth

Lucky for you, this "table" everyone talks about getting to (and that every top operating executive actually dreads being at) is a myth.

Yes, there are meetings, seminars, conferences, teleconferences, videoconferences, Zoom calls, task forces, study groups, working groups, podcast briefings, executive teams, work teams, collaborative websites, advisory committees, and boards—all populated by well-meaning, highly motivated, energetic individuals working to get things done. While each of these techniques can play a useful, often necessary role in the advancement of various organizational and business objectives, meaningful breakthroughs are made or achieved another way.

Significant progress and the crystallization of leadership aspirations are usually the work of trusted individual advisors interacting with a leader or leadership group within an organization, striving to have a constructive, measurable impact.

If you are a trusted strategic individual, you are the table. You bring the table with you. When you are in the room, the "table" is full. When you study the significant decisions leaders make, when you study successful organizations and the actions of those who lead them, you find that leaders seek out those with special insight, those with special skills and, who individually rather than collectively, provide the crucial information increments these leaders need to make significant decisions and progress.

The philosophy that underlies this book is that becoming and being a Trusted Strategic Advisor is an individual achievement and responsibility. The truth is that senior executives directly and intentionally choose those they trust to advise them on the issues that matter. Senior executives look for expertise, insight, wisdom, loyalty, commitment, and specialized knowledge as preliminary credentials for the position of trusted advisor. If the only thing you have to offer is communications advice, HR advice, legal advice, security advice, marketing advice, or financial advice, then, quite logically, that is when you will be called to help. The questions asked of you will be limited to your specific area of expertise. Once you undertake to achieve the disciplines of the Trusted Strategic Advisor—a permanent personal commitment, as described in the chapters of this book—you will experience significant individual rewards, like increased acceptance, access, impact, inclusion, influence, and most of all respect.

What matters is the constructive connection between the leader and the Trusted Strategic Advisor—the enhanced understanding and reliability that this relationship establishes, fosters, and nurtures. Remember the advice from Dan Ciampa in the beginning of your journey through this book—the three types of assistance and advice Trusted Strategic Advisors give are:

- Strategies
- Operations
- Political

You are the table because no matter how many well-meaning individuals you jam into a room, the likelihood of something productive occurring anytime soon, from the boss's perspective or as compared to your meeting with the boss alone, can go down with each additional voice present. Remember, those in the room are the boss's choice. One of the Trusted Strategic Advisor's crucial responsibilities is to help the boss find appropriate talent and available outside voices.

Most of our careers have been spent working primarily in the fields of crisis communication management and response, leadership building, reputation recovery, and strategy. One of the most powerful early lessons we learned is that when big problems occur, the best strategy is to help the boss find truly knowledgeable, experienced people who have been through similar circumstances and could guide, coach, or be a truth revealer to the boss.

Teams are or may be needed for many things—putting out fires, rebuilding relationships and facilities, as well as re-educating and sometimes rehabilitating employee and community relationships. But when recovery missions get muddled, it is the boss who gets fired rather than the advisor or staff people.

The most important step on the way to becoming a Trusted Strategic Advisor is your personal commitment to becoming one, then publicly and purposefully undertaking the steps and decisions to achieve your goal.

The Eight Key Personal Aspirations, Motivations, and Missions of a Trusted Strategic Advisor

In our decades working with senior leaders across forms of organization, we have been driven by our own aspirations, motivations, and missions. For example, Fred's mission—in his firm, in his work with clients, in his teaching, in his scholarship, and in his writing—is: Build a better world by equipping people to be leaders who ignite and inspire change in the world for the good. That's his North Star. That's how he prioritizes his time and what he chooses to focus on and to ignore.

Jim's half-century career has involved deep discernment of his own aspirations, motivations, and mission. Jim's aspirations can be universalized to other Trusted Strategic Advisors. Here's what Jim has aspired to over the course of his career, which you can share, as Fred does:

1. **Acceptance:** The automatic acknowledgment of your expertise and the value of having you involved in most conversations.
2. **Access:** Be able to knock on the door rather than waiting for the phone to ring.
3. **Having impact:** Talking, thinking, writing, and behaving in ways that are more memorable and are retained and repeated by those we counsel.

4. **Importance:** Use power language. Say things that matter and be intentionally important.
5. **Inclusion:** Condition those you advise to mention and suggest that you be included in other circles of influence because of the inherent value of the work you're currently doing and have done.
6. **Interaction and engagement in bigger ideas:** To be thought of as a go-to person when the ideas get big and more meaningful.
7. **Relevance:** We belong to a profession that has to constantly validate its relevance. My advice: Avoid all things that aren't relevant. These eight aspirations are the definition of relevance.
8. **Respect:** Trust based on truth. Being known as the person to go to for the ultimate advice and counsel, the truth needed on any given issue or topic, and to find out and tell the rest of that truth.

You may wish to add others to this list, but note that this is already a pretty powerful list of expectations and targeted behaviors on your part. It's a very management-oriented set of expectations.

Have a Personal Manifesto to Guide Your Practice

A manifesto is a public declaration of intentions, opinions, objectives, or motives. Jim has spent 50 years refining what he stands for, always searching for the truth first and helping others do the same. Fred has done the same for the nearly 40 years he has known Jim. And you can as well. We share these motives with anyone interested, but especially those whom we advise. In order to be a truly successful Trusted Strategic Advisor, you need to teach what you coach in ways that help CEOs absorb what you are talking about and do, in many cases, what you advise. You need to teach yourself right along with the advice you give.

Start building your own practice manifesto now. What will your practice manifesto look like? Here's Jim's to get you started.

Jim's Practice Manifesto:

1. Seek the truth first; find ethical, civil, and decent pathways, promptly and urgently.
2. Truth is generally best expressed in positive declarative language and consists of 15% facts and data and 85% emotion and point of reference.

There is a mistaken notion (from business schools) that the more facts presented the more likely the truth will emerge. The exact opposite is true. The more facts and data are released, the more confused people get. But more importantly, burying people, especially victims, in facts and data makes them feel stupid or foolish, and they get angrier and more powerful. The challenge of truth is understanding the emotionality of truth and especially the fact that there are different points of reference on every issue or question. In fact, there is a different point of reference for every witness, every victim, and everyone affected. Each of those points of reference is valid and true from the perspective of the person involved.

The challenge of truth is always finding significant and important factual information but understanding, interpreting, and sometimes negotiating with people whose point of reference is very different from others involved in the same issue, situation, or problem.

Management often uses facts and data as a defense against having to interpret, explore, and explain emotions. The more facts are used as weapons, the bigger your loss will be when you finally settle the issue.

3. Use truth-hiding and truth-confusing techniques very carefully. Storytelling, metaphors, allegories, euphemisms, ". . . in other words" similes, and analogies rarely reveal, explore, or produce truth. Remember, these techniques are frequently used by liars. If something is a half-truth, it is a whole lie.
4. Avoid known patterns of failure: silence, stalling, denial, victim-confusion, testosterosis, arrogance, searching for the guilty, fear of the media, whining. All of these behaviors build suspicion and anger.
5. Ask better, tougher, more constructive questions than anyone else.
6. Be 15 minutes early, or first.
7. Avoid surprises, forecast trouble (have a readiness plan in hand).
8. Think before you edit, put your pencil down. Question all edits. Resist mindless editing. Seek simple, sensible, constructive explanations and information. Effective editing makes the truth easier to see, often in fewer words.

9. Constantly challenge the standard assumptions and practices of our profession; build its importance and enhance the ability of all practitioners to better serve others from their perspective. Raise your hand. Speak up. Break the silence. Reveal the truth.
10. Be productive, do the doable; know the knowable; get the getable; arrange the arrangeable, avoid the dumb and troublesome decisions and actions you know you should. Make a list. Remember. If you make a bad decision, never repeat it.
11. Say things others fear to say, voice them first. Start with what is obvious and likely true. All crises ripen badly. In crises, things will always get worse before they can get better.
12. Say less but make it more important. Write less but make it more meaningful and memorable.
13. Go beyond what those you advise and those you work with already know or believe.
14. Intend to make constructive, positive ethical differences every day. Keep a log.
15. Intentionally look at every situation and circumstance from different, constructive, and surprising perspectives.
16. Look out for the real victims. Always put victim interests first. Fail to do this and the victims will bury you.
17. Remember, it's your boss's "bus." They get to drive it wherever they want. Your role on "the bus" is to help the driver drive better. If you don't like it, or them, can't change it, or them, hop off, find another bus, or find and drive your own.
18. Stop trying to save the day. The biggest staff mistake is to hang around in the vain belief that you can redeem yourself or change how someone powerful does things, believes, and behaves. When they are done asking you and listening to you, find a new bus. When they have an opportunity to look a new direction, they surprise you by hiring an outsider and then you're gone.
19. Remember the loyalty exception: If whatever is happening on your bus is illegal, immoral, monumentally stupid, what are you doing there anyway? Leave that bus today and find a better one, or start your own.

20. Be aware that every issue, question, concern, or problem is a management/leadership issue, question, concern, or problem (rather than a crisis) before it is any other kind of issue, question, concern, or problem (including public relations).
21. Start where leadership or management IS or you will end up in different places and fail.
22. Strive for simple, sensible, sensitive, positive, constructive, compassionate, helpful, honorable, and ethical action options. All other approaches lead to trouble.
23. The most usable advice format for leaders and managers to choose from is options. Always provide your advice as three options: doing nothing (0% option), doing something (100% option), doing something more (125% option). Let the person whose career is on the line choose the options and make the key decisions. That's their job. Your job is to identify plausible, ethical, sensible, doable options from which managers and leaders can choose.
24. Be inconsistent. Inconsistency is the greatest virtue of strategy. The strategist's greatest value is intentional inconsistency. If all you can provide are things the people around you already know, why are you there?
25. Avoid, prevent, or stop Evil, the increasingly intentional harming of innocents and people without power. Innocents include vulnerable populations, animals and living creatures, and living systems (forests, bodies of water, the earth). (See 5 below.)

Jim's Fundamental Beliefs

1. All questionable, inappropriate, unethical, unconscionable, immoral, predatory, improper, victim-producing, and criminal behaviors are intentional. Adults chose specifically to do wrong.
2. All ethical, moral, compassionate, decent, civil, and lawful behaviors are also intentional.
3. The choice is always clear and always yours.
4. Those who lead with genuine integrity, civility, respect, decency, humility, and compassion are likely to be more ethical and trustworthy.

5. Unconscionable intentions, behaviors, actions, and decisions that vilify, demean, dismiss, diminish, humiliate, cause needless but intentional pain, express anger and irritation, demand or bully, are mean, negative, insulting, disrespectful, disparaging, tone-deaf, without empathy, that intentionally injure, accuse, overbear, are punitive, restrictive, exceed the boundaries of decency, civility, and integrity, are, in my judgment, all unethical.
6. Teaching what I can do, how I can help, the perspectives I bring, this is the substance of the seventh discipline, teaching the CEO how to best utilize my skills and services. If it doesn't work or only works for a limited time, be prepared to move on, because they may have for any number of reasons.

The Trusted Strategic Advisor Is Committed To:

1. Understanding how leaders think and operate with a focus on suggesting options that can lead to solutions.
2. Recognizing and anticipating what leaders expect and experience.
3. Studying leaders and leadership to understand the patterns of thinking, decision-making, and action-taking.
4. Having a relationship with leaders built on trust and service.
5. Practicing the disciplines of the Trusted Strategic Advisor:
   a. Become a verbal visionary.
   b. Gain and maintain a management perspective.
   c. Develop a strategic mindset.
   d. Apply the power of patterns with the goal of being a forecaster.
   e. Provide sensible, constructive advice and coach the boss on how to take advantage of your wisdom.

Your Manifesto Is Your Publicly Declared but Personal List of Daily Obligations, That Will Set You Apart and Help Assure Your Success

What About You? What are the principles that guide your practice, your thinking, your actions? What does your practice manifesto look like?

We are always open to conversations about all of these ideas. You can contact Jim at jel@e911.com, subject line: "Ethical and Practical Principles." If you do contact Jim, he will send you his powerful one-page "Model Personal Profile, The Purposes and Passions of My Life."

You can contact Fred at hfgarcia@logosconsulting.net.

You're on your own (YOYO) in this quest. Be strategic. Be the table. Solution options are always your responsibility. Find the ingredients of successful strategy. Manage your own destiny by helping leaders achieve and manage theirs.

You can do this. Those who do will have a happier, important, and fulfilling professional career. See you at the top.

Please let us know what you learn along the way.

We hope you might take a shot at answering five questions about your experience with *Influencing Leaders*.

1. What is the most important thing you learned in this book? You're free to share more than one.
2. What is the most interesting thing you learned from the book *Influencing Leaders*?
3. What is the most surprising thing you learned from this book?
4. What questions were raised by this book that need answers and further conversation?
5. What are you going to do different later today and tomorrow having had the experience of working through this book?

Notes

Chapter 1

1. Kowitt, Beth. *"The New CEO Is Younger and May Even Be a Woman." Bloomberg Law*, 15 Feb. 2023.
2. McGregor, Jena. *"CEO Turnover Is Picking Up Again as the Pandemic Wanes—But Not for Poor Performance." Forbes*, 8 Sept. 2022.
3. Ciampa, Dan. *"After the Handshake." Harvard Business Review*, Dec. 2016.
4. Recounted in Ciampa, *Dan After the Handshake: The CEO's Guide to the First 100 Days* (Boston: Harvard Business School Press, 2005), 3.
5. Jeffrey R. Immelt, interview by Thomas A. Stewart, "How Jeff Immelt Runs GE," *Harvard Business Review* 87, no. 9 (September 2009): 42–49.

Chapter 2

1. David A. Nadler, "Confessions of a Trusted Counselor," *Harvard Business Review*, Sept. 2005.

Chapter 3

1. Larry Bossidy, "What Your Leader Expects of You, and What You Should Expect in Return," *Harvard Business Review* 80, no. 3 (March 2002): 58–65.

Chapter 4

1. Aaron Sorkin, *"Noël,"* The West Wing, season 2, episode 10, directed by Thomas Schlamme, aired December 20, 2000, NBC.

Chapter 5

1. Welch, Jack. and John A. Byrne. *Straight from the Gut.* Warner Books, 2001.
2. The anecdote commonly attributed to Sherlock Holmes and Dr. Watson—in which Holmes deduces that "someone has stolen our tent"—**does not appear** in The Hound of the Baskervilles or any other work by Arthur Conan Doyle. Quotation scholars classify it as a modern humorous parable illustrating inference and critical thinking. See Jan Harold Brunvand, *The Study of American Folklore* (New York: W.W. Norton, 1998), and Ralph Keyes, *The Quote Verifier* (New York: St. Martin's Press, 2006).
3. William of Ockham, *Philosophical Writings*, trans. Philotheus Boehner (Indianapolis: Hackett Publishing, 1990).
4. Franklin, Benjamin. *The Autobiography of Benjamin Franklin.*★ Edited by Leonard W. Labaree. (New Haven: Yale University Press, 1964), 148–153.

Chapter 6

1. Kissinger, Henry. *The White House Years.* (Little, Brown and Company, 1979), 49.

Chapter 7

1. Kenichi Ohmae, *The Mind of the Strategist: Business Planning for Competitive Advantage*, (New York: Penguin Business Library, 1982), ISBN 0-14-00.9128-9 (paperback), LOC 82-2567.
2. Edward de Bono, *The Use of Lateral Thinking* (London: Jonathan Cape, 1967), 8–10.

Chapter 8

1. Peter F. Drucker, quoted in Bruce Rosenstein, *Living in More Than One World: How Peter Drucker's Wisdom Can Inspire and Transform Your Life* (New York: Berrett-Koehler, 2009), 14.

Chapter 10

1. Ciampa, Dan. *Taking Advice: Getting the Most Out of Advisory Relationships* (Harvard Business School Press, 2007), 27–33.

Index

D

E

F

G

H

I

J

K

L

U

V